through each and every interaction we face in life. May you feel as blessed as I do to have Renée's book in our lives as a beautiful, timely guidebook to lead us back home to ourselves."

— Richard Miller, PhD, clinical psychologist, author of *Yoga Nidra*, and founder of Integrative Restoration Institute (iRest)

"A gift to families, this handbook for everyday spirituality is filled with practical, down-to-earth, and transformative wisdom. Renée's accessible and empowering approach provides new ways to stay connected to your true nature and help your family do the same. A must-read for peace in the midst of chaotic family life!"

— Amy McCready, founder of Positive Parenting Solutions and author of *If I Have to Tell You One More Time*

"Renée Trudeau's book gives families the support, tools, guidance, and inspiration to define *who they are* and align this with *how they live*. Empowering and encouraging, *Nurturing the Soul of Your Family* will motivate you to create the life you desire for yourself — and for your family!"

— Vicki Abeles, creator and director of the award-winning documentary *Race to Nowhere: The Dark Side of America's Achievement Culture*

Praise for *The Mother's Guide to Self-Renewal* by Renée Peterson Trudeau

"Of all the books on balance, this is the very best one. Practical, clear, and true, it invites you to engage deeply with your own experience. Only then can the superb guidance that Renée provides find its way out of your mind and into your life."

— Joan Borysenko, PhD, author of *Inner Peace for Busy Women*

"I love your book!!! Loving mothers are self-loving mothers; Renée's book informs, supports, and completely inspires this essential journey. This book is a jewel!"

— SARK, bestselling author and artist of *Glad No Matter What* and *Succulent Wild Woman*

NURTURING the SOUL of YOUR FAMILY

NURTURING
the SOUL of
YOUR FAMILY
10 Ways to Reconnect and
Find Peace in Everyday Life

RENÉE PETERSON
TRUDEAU

New World Library
Novato, California

New World Library
14 Pamaron Way
Novato, California 94949

Text design by Tona Pearce Myers

Library of Congress Cataloging-in-Publication Data
Trudeau, Renée Peterson, date.
 Nurturing the soul of your family : 10 ways to reconnect and find peace in everyday life / Renée Peterson Trudeau.
     p.   cm.
 Includes bibliographical references and index.
 ISBN 978-1-60868-158-7 (pbk. : alk. paper)—ISBN 978-1-60868-159-4 (ebook) (print)
 1. Families. 2. Interpersonal relations. 3. Work-life balance. I. Title.
 HQ734.T848 2013
 306.85—dc23   2012041213

First printing, February 2013
ISBN 978-1-60868-158-7
Printed in Canada on 100% postconsumer-waste recycled paper

New World Library is proud to be a Gold Certified Environmentally Responsible Publisher. Publisher certification awarded by Green Press Initiative. www.greenpressinitiative.org

10 9 8 7 6 5 4 3 2 1

To my six siblings — Kert, Geoffrey, Shiva Sean, Nathan, Teresa, and Timothy — and their life partners. When one of us heals a part of ourselves, we all heal. May we continue to support and uplift one another and remember each day who we really are.

And to my nephews, Aidan, Luca, Grayson, and Guthrie, and my niece, Fiona Grace — thank you for choosing our tribe. The gift of your presence blesses us all. ·

"When you do things from your soul,
you feel a river moving in you, a joy."

— Jelaluddin Rumi

CONTENTS

PART IV: EXPLORE A NEW WAY OF BEING

PART V: FIND YOUR TRIBE, EMBRACE SUPPORT

Introduction

A CALL for a NEW WAY of BEING

It's 6:45 Monday morning. Your kids are arguing over the iPad, and your phone keeps chiming with new messages. You feel exhausted and overwhelmed; things are moving too fast. Your weekend was a blur of activity, and now you watch your distracted partner rush out the door to work as you make lunches and get the kids ready for their day. You glance at your weekly calendar, overflowing with appointments and kids' activities, and your chest tightens. Everyone seems to be moving in different directions at once. You crave a slower, simpler, more spacious life. You long to feel more connected to your family and to experience more peace and harmony in the everyday. But it feels like too much work, too impossible. You're not even sure where to begin.

Nurturing the Soul of Your Family is a call to explore a new way of being. It's an invitation to live an awakened life in the midst of the ordinary tasks of everyday living. It's a guidebook to help you and your family learn to nurture your hearts and souls by slowing down, reconnecting, and beginning to live the life you desire.

An infinite river of well-being runs through each of us. Whether we call it God, our intuition, or a higher power, it's innate, true, and wise. It's always present, ready to guide and restore us. When we consciously choose to return to this source, we feel connected to everyone and everything around us — life flows. But we need reminders that this ever-present wisdom exists, waiting to be tapped. It's our birthright to feel good and to be able to access this sense of peace — no matter how crazy things around us may get.

This book was created to help you stay connected to — and live from — this source and to support you in helping those you love do the same.

OUR DESIRE for CHANGE

We live today with unprecedented levels of change and uncertainty. During the past twelve years, I've coached thousands of men and women from their thirties to their sixties, and several dominant themes have emerged. Here are some of the ways my clients have characterized their challenges and desires:

- "I crave community — real community, heartfelt connection, and meaningful dialogue."
- "Things are moving too fast. I feel overscheduled and overextended. I want more space in my life, more time to just be. And I know my kids and partner want this, too!"
- "Since losing my job and wrangling with all the economic uncertainty, I feel like I'm in limbo. I'm so tired of living in the unknown."
- "I'm stretched so thin. I don't feel successful at work or in my family life. I'm just paddling to keep my head above water."
- "I often wonder how I ended up where I am. In hindsight, I did what I thought I was 'supposed' to do. I'm now realizing I'm not living the life I desire, so whose life is this?"
- "I feel like I've created a monster. I'm working really hard to pay for a lifestyle and home that leave me with very little freedom, time, or financial breathing room!"
- "I'm depressed or anxious a lot of the time. I feel like I've lost that joie de vivre, like the 'joy train' is passing me by."

- "I'm craving meaning and spirituality in my life, but I have no idea what this looks like or where to begin. My religious upbringing turned me off to 'God' and left me wondering what I truly believe."

As I was writing this book, I surveyed hundreds of families through the Personal Renewal Groups (PRGs) that I've developed. I created PRGs after the birth of my son, as a response to my personal need for self-nurturance and based on my first book, *The Mother's Guide to Self-Renewal*. PRGs are self-renewal circles for mothers, and they are now led by trained facilitators worldwide. I asked participants to share what derails their family's emotional and spiritual well-being. The predominant themes mirrored those voiced by my clients:

- the overuse and misuse of technology, or feeling plugged in 24/7;
- being too busy, overscheduled, always rushing from one thing to the next;
- losing the ability to find joy in family life;
- letting things that matter least take precedence over things that matter most; and
- Mom and Dad not taking time for self-care and parenting from an empty cup.

As we navigate and raise families in this crazy-busy disconnected world, how do we enhance our emotional well-being and experience more harmony in our everyday moments? What would this look like?

A SHIFT in PERSPECTIVE

Imagine experiencing more simplicity and spaciousness in your life — in how you think, work, parent, and connect to those you love. Imagine your family as your greatest source of joy. Imagine having the ability to transform and more easily navigate the challenges you face each day, so you feel less hurried and rushed. Envision a life that is slower, more relaxed — with plenty of time for those things that matter most. Imagine embracing a new way of being in the world that supports you in experiencing more trust and flow and happiness.

As parents, we focus so much attention on our kids' academic and physical development. Imagine devoting that same level of energy to nurturing their hearts and spirits, so that our family's emotional and spiritual well-being is the top priority. Imagine exploring how to truly nurture our soul and the soul of our family in order to awaken to a deeper level of connection — to ourselves and others?

Just for a minute shift your perspective and picture your family as a sacred tribe. Think of your loved ones as a carefully chosen collective of souls who have joined — not by accident, but intentionally — for an important reason: to support one another's collective growth. Does that change how you see things and how you relate to them?

Everything we truly desire — love, connection, meaning, purpose, joy — is available to us right here, right now, through the people we live, eat, and sleep with every day.

MY TEACHERS, MY CLASSROOM

It's 1984, and I'm sitting in my cold, third-floor dorm room. The door is locked; the room feels small. Down the hall I can hear the whirring of blenders, Bruce Springsteen on the stereo, and girls yelling, running from room to room preparing for a sixties-themed dorm party that evening.

I'm eighteen, a freshman in college. I have just received a call from my paternal grandmother. My forty-four-year-old father is in intensive care. He's had a massive heart attack. Worse, it turns out that my self-employed dad's office manager forgot to pay his health and life insurance premiums, and this news has sent my mother over the edge. She has been taken to a mental hospital. Meanwhile, my six siblings, ranging in age from four to seventeen, are... God only knows.

I want to vomit. My body feels frozen. I don't know whether to cry, jump in my car and drive home to San Antonio, or bury my head under the covers of my faded pink comforter. Finals week starts in ten hours.

Numb with pain, I eat some chocolate chip cookies as my thoughts and nervous system spiral out of control.

In my wild, highly creative, and adventurous upbringing, chaos and uncertainty were constant companions, and childhood experiences like this inspired me to pursue the work I'm doing now: *helping families awaken and access their innate well-being.* I believe that it's our birthright to experience a safe, loving, communicative environment that provides everyone — parents and kids alike — with the nourishment and support we need to bravely head out in the world to do our work. It also satisfies our deep yearning and desire for unshakable inner peace.

I was born in Houston, Texas, in 1966, the oldest of seven children. My youngest siblings — a pair of boy/girl twins — were an unplanned "surprise" who arrived shortly after my mother's fortieth birthday. I was then fourteen, and by the time I left for college four years later, I had changed thousands of diapers.

My mother was a gifted artist and musician, but she suffered from clinical depression, which arrived on the wings of postpartum blues just after the birth of her second child, my oldest brother. At that time, we were stationed in Japan during the Vietnam War, since my father, a physician, was paying his dues to the Air Force for putting him through medical school. I was fourteen months old when this dark visitor first came knocking.

My dad was an intellectual, generous man, but he was constantly in his head. Perhaps he retreated there to make sense of all the crazy activity of his seven children. Much of the time it felt like we were the Swiss Family Robinson, questing for solid ground, looking for clear guidance and anchors, yet swimming in a sea of uncertainty.

My childhood was an emotional roller coaster. My parents both came from families with histories of alcoholism, depression, addiction, heart disease and diabetes, infidelity, and divorce. They used to joke that they had no business having children — let alone seven of us! They did the best they could, though, to create a healthy family dynamic. They were always experimenting with new parenting modalities and approaches. They just didn't have the support or the tools needed to create consistency. The baggage from their own childhoods and marriage was, I believe, just too overwhelming, heavy, and difficult for them to let Goodwill haul it all away. Like many of us, they were a bit lost and unsure how to find their way home.

Yet along with the pain, loss, disconnection, and missteps, our family provided many beautiful gifts.

When we were kids, our creativity was nourished daily. There was an unwavering focus on spiritual nourishment and how we connect to the Divine. We were exposed to many unique cultural and educational experiences. We feasted on art and music; we were encouraged to be very independent, to try new things, to make mistakes, and to find our own path in the world. I recall friends' parents quizzing us when we would come over for a play date: "So your parents actually let you loose in the kitchen to cook *alone*? And you go to what kind of school again?"

Growing up, I fought a lot with my brother Kert. When this happened, my dad would stop what he was doing, call us over, and ask us to look each other in the eye. Then he'd say, "You are flesh of my flesh, blood of my blood, and you'll always have each other. Remember this."

I would roll my eyes at this dramatic statement and count the seconds until I could pull away. What I believe he sensed on a deep level — and tried to find validation for through his study of family-centric religions like Catholicism — is how sacred the family experience is. Families don't come together by accident. They aren't science experiments that might go well or awry. We're here to consciously grow, learn, expand, and support one another's spiritual and personal growth.

THE INVITATION to AWAKEN

I believe the deep connection available to us through our family experience is sacred. Our spouse and our children are not just people we share laundry duty and cereal with; they are wise souls and fellow sojourners who happen to be in human bodies.

Everything you want to experience with your family you already possess. There's no need to create, craft, cook, farm, buy, or become something new in order to experience what's available to you in the now, in everyday moments. Our family presents us with the opportunity to come into the highest expression of who we are and to experience giving and receiving love in profound and numerous ways.

We underestimate how well equipped we are to do this. And how wise we are.

The external world tells us that happiness is "out there." If we just work hard enough to figure it out, read the right books, strive harder for our goals, and outmaneuver our circumstances — we'll get there. Someday.

This couldn't be further from the truth.

Everything in our being is innately wired to support us in returning to greater harmony and equilibrium, individually and collectively. A revered yoga teacher once told me each of us has thousands of internal systems within our physiology that work continually to bring us back to our natural state of balance. We already possess the innate ability to create this harmony within our family — in fact, we are born with it. We just have to consciously choose to access it.

> *"The minute you begin to do what you want to do, it's a different kind of life."*
> — R. Buckminster Fuller

It's time to wake up from this bad dream of continual dis-ease and dis-connection and to consciously craft and embrace a life we love, not one we simply endure.

It takes tremendous courage and desire to live an awakened life: a life where your actions are in alignment with your deepest values, where you're making decisions that support your family's emotional and spiritual well-being. Is there anything more important? Is there ever a better time than now?

THE HARDEST JOB on the PLANET

It's 1976, I'm in fifth grade, and I'm standing by the front door, shouldering my backpack, my eyes darting, watching my family scamper like mice from room to room. My stomach is in knots. It's 7:45 A.M. We should have left fifteen minutes ago. Lunches are half-made, my brothers are shooting with slingshots at each other, and my mom — never a morning person — is withdrawn, in a bad mood, and admonishing my dad (our morning chauffeur) about forgetting to pay a bill. I'm filled with anxiety and frustration; my nervous system is shot from all the noise and stress. We finally arrive at school, and the VW van door opens. My siblings and I roll out and run off to our different classrooms with barely a wave — I look back for a minute and see my dad hunched over the wheel eating Grape-Nuts out of a tall, glass measuring cup before starting the car again. His jaw is clenched, and his brow is knit with worry and stress.

Today, I'm a parent. While I do my best to try to keep our mornings peaceful, sometimes they turn into the same kind of three-ring circus — as my son frantically finishes his latest school project and I navigate a business deadline while rescheduling a forgotten dentist appointment, and so on.

One morning several years ago, after a particularly rough start with my then-seven-year-old son, I dropped by his school to deliver an apology note to him. A short while later, his teacher, Deborah, left me a voice-mail message letting me know how deeply my son had been moved by the card. She said they had both shared some tears, and she doubted he would ever forget this action. Knowing mornings are key for setting the tone for the day, I couldn't bear for either of us to begin our day with that much stress! My upbringing left a huge imprint on how I view morning time. That voice-mail message is still saved on my phone to this day.

Many of us are asking, "Where did all the fun go?! I thought having a family was supposed to enhance my life, to offer opportunities for joy and delight! When did things start becoming so tedious? So involved, so complex, so overwhelming? So darn hard?!"

Having children and raising a family is the hardest job on the planet. Give me a challenging client over negotiating media time with my disgruntled adolescent any day! We're ready for a new way. Not a new technique, smart phone app, or the discipline approach du jour, but a real breakthrough. This book offers a chance to start over, to start fresh and really envision, claim, and step into a new way of being.

I once heard Richard Louv, author of *Last Child in the Woods: Saving Our Children from Nature Deficit Disorder*, speak at my local bookstore. He believes one problem many of us have is that we don't envision or imagine a great future. We don't know what it would look like for us. He says when people are asked to envision the future, many describe a teched-out, overdigitized, virtual world in which we're even less connected than we are now (like *Blade Runner*)! Author and futurist Barbara Marx Hubbard, in her documentary *Humanity Ascending*, says that it's crucial for us to envision who we want to be as a people and how we want to use all these gifts and powers that we've developed.

If we don't consciously create the future we desire, we may end up creating something no one wants.

Over the years, my coaching clients have shared that one of the biggest gifts they receive is the opportunity to be challenged to imagine what is possible in their lives and careers: to shed the shackles of their expectations, to dump their old, crunchy, outdated ways of being in the world, and to start anew.

This book presents you with the same challenging question: What would a new way of being look like? What would it look like for you — and your family — to be more conscious, more connected? How do you picture interacting, sharing, and loving right now, and what will this look like when your kids leave the nest? What would your family relationships look like if you stepped into the highest expression of who you are?

To help you answer these questions, this book guides you in exploring the most powerful, essential things you can do right now to bring more peace and harmony to your family, or what I consider the ten paths to peace. I hope this book will help you realize you *do* have the answers you need. You just have to become quiet enough — and create the space — to hear them.

The ten paths to peace mirror the chapter titles. They are:

- Tapping the transformative power of self-care: attune and respond to your needs and desires
- Healing from the inside out: peace begins with me
- Unplugging to plug in: remember, people first, things second
- Unleashing the healing power of nature: the ultimate antidepressant
- Making time for spiritual renewal: return to the river within
- Loving the ones you're with: spend time together (like you mean it!)

- Defining, celebrating, and honoring your family culture: what do you stand for?
- Slowing down: do less to experience more
- Exploring a new way of being: make hard choices, break free, and do it different
- Building your tribe: ask for and embrace help as you create your support network

These paths to peace are integral to, and they support and build on, one another. I encourage you to read and approach them in the order in which they're presented, but as always, listen to your intuition on how best to explore these teachings.

A CALLING to LIVE INSIDE OUT

When my brother Geoffrey was twenty, he committed suicide; in hindsight, we believe he was probably battling adult-onset schizophrenia. When my gentle, artistic brother left us, the heart of our family was shattered and ran in eight different directions, like mercury hitting a cold bathroom floor.

Four years later my dad died at fifty-six; my mom followed him four years later at age sixty. Both passed suddenly and unexpectedly from heart ailments. I don't think they ever recovered or healed from the heartache of losing Geoffrey. If my mom and dad could have received the support they needed and were reminded of their innate wisdom, I believe it would have radically shifted the culture of our family.

I wrote this book as a call to explore how we can "live inside out." That is, live in alignment with what matters most and with intention — as opposed to moving through life as if we're in a never-ending tennis match, frantically reacting to whatever is thrown at us.

When our sense of inner peace grows, external conflicts dissipate. When we begin to cultivate and return to our inner state of harmony and our river of well-being, we're able to be less reactive and more present, calm, and heart centered.

Having worked with thousands of parents, I've observed that when parents take time to nurture themselves, their families naturally come into greater equilibrium. Cancer survivor Audre Lorde said, "Self-care is not about self-indulgence, it's about self-preservation."

Relationships improve when we enhance our state of emotional well-being and perspective. We can't change others, but we shift the dynamic when we awaken and are willing to work on our own healing. This first became clear to me when I traveled to San Antonio in my early twenties to visit my mother. Afterward, it would take me weeks to recover emotionally from our draining, sometimes toxic encounters. My slow, painful disentanglement from this key relationship began when I finally understood where the opportunity for change really lay — with me.

In our wise moments as parents, we observe and know that we have an enormous impact on the day-to-day "ride" we experience with our families. Will the day be a mile-high carnival roller coaster or will it be a playful river cruise?

Our kids' behavior is inextricably tied to our emotional well-being. If things around us are in disequilibrium or are out of sync, we need to have the courage to examine if *we're* in disequilibrium. What's going on with our inner world, our lens, and how we're viewing life in general? Often this becomes a wake-up call to begin to parent more consciously and to explore if a course correction is needed on our part.

In my life-coaching work, I've observed that we all desire three things:

- to know we're heard and we matter,
- to feel loved and have opportunities to express our love, and
- to feel like we belong and have a tribe we can count on for support.

Each family has its own beautiful, unique essence or sacred connection. Just as we need to tend to the emotional well-being of any relationship in order for it to thrive, we have to consciously nourish and nurture our family's sweet, tender soul. What type of daily care, feeding, and love does your family's essence need in order to grow strong and soar?

When your family is feeling disconnected, stuck, or at odds — and since we're all human, this will happen a lot — don't just swallow the pill fed to us by TV sitcoms that this is how family life is. Pause. Be willing to open up to other possibilities. Then practice new ways of seeing and being.

THE TIME IS NOW

Challenge your beliefs about being in a family and about being in relationship. Cultivate a sense of curiosity. Ask: What if? Could there be another way? Is it possible I'm seeing this situation from a distorted view? What is my role in this experience? What am I bringing to the relationship? A wise grounded parenting coach told me the most important feeling we can cultivate when relating to our children and exploring our family's interactions is *curiosity*.

There is no greater spiritual work than conscious parenting and agreeing to live with other beings on this level of intimacy. My brother Kert once told me, "Relationships are mirrors for our own stuff. It's much easier to be alone. But if you want to really grow, sign up for a relationship. Intimacy is not for the faint of heart."

More than anything, we all crave connection and community. This starts at home, and it starts right now — not a month or year from now. Now is the time to awaken, heal, open our hearts, and reconnect with the most important people we'll ever know. This book is an invitation to begin your journey. Know you're not alone; we're in this together.

Grab a notebook and pen, keep an open mind and heart, and let's explore what it would look like to embrace a new way of being as we proceed slowly, with a sense of curiosity and lots of self-compassion. Let's begin!

HOW to GET the MOST from THIS BOOK

Most of all, read with the utmost self-compassion — be gentle with yourself. Family work doesn't always come naturally, and at some point you will probably experience strong feelings. So, slip on your lab coat, pick up a clipboard and pen, and observe yourself thoughtfully and with a sense of playful curiosity. Be prepared to be surprised, and expect an occasional conflict or the experience of "contrast." Finally, regard this book as a grand feast or a buffet: some things you will find delectable, some may not be your cup of tea, and some you may develop a taste for over time. This is all part of the process as you sort through where your family is now and where you want to be.

In addition, keep in mind the following:

- At the beginning of each chapter is a "Pause for Peace." These are body-centered exercises to help calm and ground you as you ease into each theme.

- At the end of each chapter is a "Pat on the Back: What's Working?" section. We often don't give enough credit where it's due and are way too hard on ourselves. This section is a prompt to acknowledge everything you're doing for yourself and your family that is working.

- Each chapter ends with an important "Putting It into Practice" exercise. After absorbing the chapter's insights and ideas, you'll be challenged to take action and engage in an activity tied to the chapter theme. These exercises provide a powerful opportunity to come into greater alignment with the life you desire — create time for these.

- To assist your reflections, each chapter also ends with the guided journaling prompt "Imagine a New Way of Being." These provide questions to help you envision what's possible for you and your family. But at all times, keep asking, "What if..." Beautiful shifts are born from the space of possibility and potential.

- Be willing to roll up your sleeves and step out of your comfort zone. Real change comes when we "do it different" — when we stretch and try something new, even if it's a little scary.

- Tread slowly: if you only embraced one of these ideas, that alone could make a huge impact on your day-to-day experience. Big shifts often begin with baby steps.

- Find your tribe: ask for and receive support and build your team. Know that there are thousands of other families out there who, just like you, are ready to birth a new way of being! Also, consider joining a Personal Renewal Group (for more, see chapter 1 and visit www.ReneeTrudeau.com).

Part I

HEAL YOURSELF, HEAL YOUR FAMILY

PAUSE for PEACE
A Self-Care Checkup

Take a moment to close your eyes, slowly scan your body,
and check in with how you're feeling. Ask, *What do I most need
to feel nurtured and to function at my best today — emotionally, physically, mentally, and spiritually?* Respond to whatever comes up: maybe
it's saying no to a commitment, altering your schedule for the day, asking for a shoulder massage, going for a walk, cutting back on caffeine or
sugar, getting more sleep, taking weekly solo dates, finding a therapist or
coach for support around a difficult issue, or going to dinner with a friend
you haven't seen in a while. Don't question what arises; just listen and
respond. Doing regular self-care checkups each morning — ideally
before you get out of bed — sends a message to your heart and soul
that you're committed to your well-being. Your life will begin
to change radically once you start to feel loved, nurtured,
and truly in tune with your own needs. Everyone
will benefit!

Chapter 1

THE TRANSFORMATIVE POWER of SELF-CARE

One day when my son was in preschool, I was filled with gratitude for my life circumstances, and in a moment of supreme clarity I wrote:

> *The life I desire is marked by deep connections to my child and partner. It's a life filled with joy and meaning. It's a life in which I feel supported and nurtured by an incredible community of men and women — young and old. I experience regular, meaningful, heartfelt connections with people I care about. I am continually open to growth — as a woman, a mother, a partner, and a spiritual being. I enjoy supporting and serving others in a way that feeds me rather than drains me. I feel that I always have enough time in my life for those things that are most important to me. My life flows, I trust my intuition, and I expect good to come to me. I feel peaceful. I am loving, and I feel loved. This is the life I desire.*

I was finally able to articulate this only after I became a mother, began my self-care journey, and truly started to connect to my needs and desires. My earliest recollection of ignoring my basic needs occurred when I was around ten, during one of my family's harried morning scenes.

Breakfast at our house was like a scene from the *Lucille Ball Show*. My mom was always scrambling to make lunches, my dad was running around looking for misplaced tennis shoes, my youngest siblings were racing through the house playing superheroes, and one sibling or another was usually experimenting in the kitchen — cooking peanut butter oatmeal, rice-flour pineapple muffins, or some other creative concoction. In our family, we were heartily encouraged to master life skills, which led to lots of cooking experiments and culinary mayhem in the kitchen!

One morning, my nine-year-old brother Kert, now a macrobiotic chef, was making pecan waffles for breakfast. As I reached over the waffle maker to help myself to breakfast, I bumped the edge of the hot grill and burned my elbow. I didn't mention the accident to my parents — probably because they were too distracted getting my siblings out the door to school — but hours later, I was sitting in church at the Catholic school I attended trying to ignore the pain from a small, brown, bubbly looking burn on my elbow. Rather than go to a teacher for help or a bandage, I endured the discomfort, thinking, *It's not really important enough to bother anyone. I'll be fine.*

When I was growing up, self-care was not something that was promoted or honored in my family, even though my parents were medical professionals! I had to learn this on my own.

SELF-CARE: BEYOND MASSAGES and PEDICURES

When you think about self-care, do you have visions of massages or pedicures and facials? Physical self-care is a big part of the overall picture. But total self-care also includes eliminating self-criticism, not overscheduling, releasing the need to be perfect, saying no, refusing to do things out of guilt, and giving yourself much-needed rest and downtime to refuel. Learning to attune and respond to your needs and desires — practicing self-care —

impacts every aspect of your life. Nurturing yourself is not selfish — it's essential to your survival and well-being.

My friend Erin, a self-employed mom and busy parent of two, recently shared how frustrated she was feeling. Exhausted from staying up until 2 A.M. to do laundry, she had skipped breakfast and lunch, was surviving on nothing but coffee, and had been beating herself up all day about not getting a homemade meal over to her neighbor, who had recently lost her father. As she and I visited, it dawned on us that we would never imagine denying our children sleep or nourishment, being judgmental of them, or allowing them to ignore their emotional needs. Yet, as parents, we often do this to ourselves on a daily basis.

> "Learning to attune and respond to your needs and desires — practicing self-care — impacts every aspect of your life. Nurturing yourself is not selfish — it's essential to your survival and well-being."
> — Renée Trudeau

The same love, gentle care, and compassion we offer so generously to our little ones should be extended to ourselves as well. Regardless of what we tell our children, we teach them about self-worth and how to honor oneself through our actions, not our words. Child-development experts tell us that modeling self-love and self-acceptance is the most effective way to influence our children's self-esteem and how they view themselves.

What qualifies as self-care? I define self-care as *the art of attuning and responding to your deepest needs and desires*. This will look vastly different for each of us. More than anything, it's about cultivating a new mindset in which we slow down, tune inward, and respond to what we need most in the moment. Self-care could be asking for help, doing less, taking a nap, or having lunch with a friend. As parents of infants know, even taking a shower or going to the bathroom when you need to is a form of self-care!

Listed below are examples of self-care for each aspect of your life: physical, emotional, mental, spiritual. They are suggestions for how you can nurture yourself and make self-renewal part of your everyday life. They are not a definitive list of activities you must complete. Indeed, as your children age and you enter new life stages, self-care activities change and may vary greatly.

If you were to focus on just one area, which one calls to you most right now?

PHYSICAL CARE

- Nourish your body by staying hydrated and eating healthy and energizing foods that make you feel great.
- Get enough sleep, take naps, and build in time for rest.
- Exercise to replenish your energy and manage stress.
- Take time to enjoy and appreciate your body: take a hot aromatherapy bath or give yourself a foot massage.

EMOTIONAL CARE

- Have a heart-to-heart conversation with a close friend or mentor.
- Have kind and loving thoughts about yourself: try not criticizing yourself for one week.
- Seek out support from a therapist, coach, social worker, or counselor.
- Write down your feelings and thoughts in a journal.
- Go on a fun date alone or with your partner, or organize a monthly girls' night out.

SPIRITUAL CARE

- Take time to be by yourself to think or write.
- Take a walk in a park or out in nature.
- Meditate, pray, or just reflect on what you're grateful for.
- Do something creative: paint, draw, dance, or sing.
- Volunteer for a cause you're passionate about.

MENTAL CARE

- Read a good book or see an intellectually stimulating movie.
- Develop a favorite hobby or skill or receive training in a professional area.
- Participate in a class, group, or workshop on a topic that interests you.
- Challenge yourself to learn something new — get out of your comfort zone.

BARRIERS to SELF-CARE

As a rule, our society does not honor or promote self-care, particularly for mothers — who are fed such "ideals" as "Good mothers always put their families first," "Motherhood is pure bliss," "You just have to let your body go when you become a mom," and "Good mothers are completely selfless."

These beliefs run deep — even if we don't accept them on a conscious level — and they can have a profound impact on how we view our roles as women and mothers. Realize this and be aware that the concept of self-care may feel foreign and difficult to embrace at first, to say the least!

Last year I spoke to a group of career coaches about self-care. When I encouraged them to take some time for themselves each week, they agreed they really needed to, but then they each offered a list of reasons why they couldn't: "I just don't have the time, the money, the family support, the space on my calendar," and so on. Others simply agreed and then looked down at their feet or across the room, as if I'd suggested they climb Mount Everest.

In our Personal Renewal Groups for moms, women are asked to voice what they perceive as the barriers to self-care. Some say they are afraid others will see them as selfish or otherwise bad moms if they put their needs first. Some feel they shouldn't really need self-care. Others say they don't have the time or money for self-care activities, while some dismiss their value. Some feel, regardless of the benefits, self-care will just become one more thing to add to their to-do list and worry about. Last, but most important, most hold an underlying belief that they are not worthy of self-care. They feel they don't deserve to make their needs a priority.

"Realizing that sometimes we needed togetherness and sometimes separateness changed our lives. Tuning in to what's needed individually and collectively for our family helped us all feel happier and more free."
— Alyson, 39, mother of three

To successfully implement a self-care practice, you have to dig deep, engage your heart, and ask yourself, "What is my personal motivation for self-care? Why does this matter to me, and how will it positively impact my relationship to myself and with my family?" The answers will be different for each of us. But if you truly want to experience a shift in your behavior and perspective, the motivation has to come from the inside out. For many women, prioritizing self-care is radical, since it runs counter to a culture that doesn't reward or value women (or parents) for putting their needs first. Most people understand that self-care makes good sense. We understand its importance on an intellectual level. But taking action is different. For real change to take place, you've got to dig deep and answer, "What is my highest vision for myself, and am I willing to do what's necessary to get there? Am I willing — when necessary — to put myself first?"

Recently, two of my girlfriends took extended breaks from their families while their husbands were traveling with their young kids. When I ran into them during their time alone, they were absolutely glowing. They had a sense of levity, vitality, and joy that I hadn't witnessed in a long time. It wasn't that they were leading miserable lives or didn't love being around their kids, but the break helped them recharge, reconnect to their essence, and enjoy the incredible gifts that come from listening — and responding — to our needs.

When was the last time you took a break from your family and from being a parent — whether it was for thirty minutes or three days?

"I got so tired of saying 'hurry up' to my kids all the time. I realized I needed to take time to breathe, stretch, plan my day better, and do some preparation so we weren't so rushed. When I was calm on the inside, our day flowed and was definitely less stressful."
— Kristen, 44, mother of twins

WHY SELF-CARE?

Take a moment to think about some of the reasons that self-care is important for you. How would you benefit by making time for it? Be specific, and use the list below as inspiration, particularly when you feel pressured to forgo self-care or too exhausted to follow through. Over the years of leading retreats and women's circles, I've seen and experienced a number of benefits:

- We feel more generous and can avoid building resentments toward others who demand our energy and time.

- We validate and honor our own worth, which in turn enhances true confidence and self-esteem.
- We feel alive and whole, so we are able to function at our best and do all the things we want to do.
- We renew and restore our energy and create energy reserves so we're able to weather unforeseen challenges more easily.
- We feel more loving and gentle toward ourselves, which helps us to be more present and calm and to respond wisely, intuitively, and effectively in any circumstance.
- We own our personal power and begin to realize our potential; the more self-accepting we become, the more self-assured we are.
- We feel more loving and playful, which makes us better friends, partners, and parents and more fun to be around!
- We experience heightened well-being and vitality.

The journey to making self-care a priority and understanding how life altering it can be is an evolutionary process. It takes time. Society often equates self-care with selfishness, and undoing this judgment within oneself usually happens gradually.

Each of us must make a huge paradigm shift to make self-care an every-day practice. I grew up with a mother who suffered from depression and struggled constantly with low self-worth and self-esteem, and this has motivated me to make self-care an important part of my life so I can model this behavior for my son. I want him to see the value of practicing self-care and how it can positively impact how he feels about himself and others.

Late one afternoon, when he was seven years old, my son called out to me from his bedroom, "Come play with me, Mom." I paused for a minute as I walked out of my home office and stopped at his doorway; various responses crossed my mind before I landed in my truth: "Not right now, sweetie. I had a really hard day and need to take a few minutes for myself before we begin making dinner." He looked up at me, sighed, and went back to reading his book. As I headed to my room to rest, I remembered Audre Lorde and thought, *Self-care isn't an act of selfishness, it's self-preservation, and it's as vital as oxygen is to my well-being.* I allowed myself to exhale and release any residue of guilt.

For a brief moment, I imagined my son as a college student, an adult, a lover, a husband, a father. He would need to practice self-care when he grew into all those roles, not only for himself, but for all the people in his life.

HOW SELF-CARE AFFECTS OUR PARENTING

One of the biggest benefits of a self-care practice is that it supports us in being more present with our partner and children. When we're present with those around us, we're able to experience openness, connection, joy, playfulness, spontaneity, compassion, empathy, gratitude, wisdom, and enhanced communication.

In *Slowing Down to the Speed of Life*, authors Richard Carlson and Joseph Bailey share that several serious consequences follow when your tank is empty, you're out of sync with your needs, and you're engaging in busy-minded, speeded-up parenting. To quote their book:

- "You become habitually reactive instead of responsive
- You take negative behavior personally rather than seeing the innocence
- Little events become front-page news
- You miss the good times
- You lose sight of your compassion
- You expect too much from your children"

We live in a 24/7 culture that is manically focused on multitasking and productivity. Most of us were never taught that *being* is just as important as *doing*. Slowing down and cultivating an appreciation for "being" is a new orientation. But ultimately, don't we all want to teach our kids that we value *who they are over what they do*?

Becoming attuned to your needs and what feeds you and creating space to nurture yourself don't happen overnight. Once you taste the benefits of self-care, however, you begin to appreciate the payoffs. Eventually, your mindset changes: you schedule time for self-nurturing just as you schedule doctor or dentist appointments. You discover that self-care is integral to your emotional survival and that you are wiser and more effective in all areas of your life when you take time to fill your cup first.

Jennifer, a self-employed writer and mom to twins, shared with me: "The other night at dinner my husband commented on how much more relaxed and joyful I seemed since I had started exercising and taking 'journaling dates.' And since I started taking time for me, I also feel more generous and playful with my kids. Connecting with my needs has had a big impact on my parenting."

The changes Jennifer made in her life inspired her husband to focus on his self-care, and now he takes guitar classes every Wednesday night. Jennifer uses that evening to connect with other moms whose partners also claim Wednesday night for their solo dates. The women have dubbed these regular dinners out with the kids the "Wednesday Night Dinner Club"; everyone now looks forward to and relishes these weekly community gatherings.

When we practice self-care, sometimes our parenting starts to look different than we may have been trained to expect. As we begin to make self-care a priority, it's important to cultivate self-acceptance and, when needed, to practice "good is good enough" parenting. For myself, as a recovering perfectionist and control freak, I slowly came to realize that working on releasing self-critical thoughts and easing my unreasonably high expectations of myself — particularly regarding parenting and motherhood — were the kindest form of self-care possible.

When my friend Lisa shared with her mother-in-law, Rose, what she was working on in her self-renewal circle — taking time for self-renewal and reconnecting with her desires and needs — Rose's eyes welled up with tears. She told Lisa, "I wish I had taken time for myself when I was raising my boys. Honestly, I just felt so overwhelmed by all the crazy expectations I placed on myself during that time, it was hard for me to focus on much else. Because of all that, a lot of the time I was depressed, unhappy, and disconnected from myself and my family."

Taking a stand for your needs and making your self-renewal a priority takes courage, committing to a road less traveled, and a willingness to live from the inside out.

SELF-CARE = LIVING INSIDE OUT

Self-care is the foundation for becoming a courageous parent. It's not about pampering; it's about owning your personal power. It's about self-worth and honoring the person you are. I believe this is our spiritual birthright.

More than ever, thousands of us are hitting the pause button and reflecting on what's really important in life. We're realizing our external environment can change on a dime. We're seeing how essential it is that our actions, words, thoughts, and parenting decisions align with our internal wisdom and core values.

When you allow your inner landscape to be as big as your outer landscape, your life will begin to change in radical, positive ways. Living from the inside out can look different for each of us, but these are some essential aspects:

- Living and parenting more intentionally and creating circumstances that support you in responding rather than always reacting to events and crises.
- Living a life that is driven by internal values, as opposed to external or societal values; this means listening to your wise self, following your heart, trusting your intuition, and caring for yourself regardless of what others may think.
- Living from a place of peace and love rather than a place of fear, and making decisions from a place of compassion rather than judgment.
- Slowing down and saying no to what drains you, so you can say yes to what matters most.
- Pausing to recognize your needs and desires; asking for and allowing yourself to receive help.
- Practicing self-compassion and being gentle with yourself.

My favorite quote from Goethe is taped to my computer: "Things which matter most must never be at the mercy of things which matter least." Surround yourself with reminders to connect with and nurture your needs. Support is essential. Take time to consciously build a community of friends, colleagues, and mentors who also believe in the transformative power of self-care.

How parents respond to and practice the art of self-care affects the entire family's well-being. Having grown up with a mother who struggled with self-acceptance all her life, I know this down to my bones. When a mother feels that her needs matter and are being met, when she begins to understand that she's more than a taskmaster, and when she starts to *like* and hopefully, in time, *love* herself, the effect on her immediate family, extended family, and community is enormous.

We are all affected by one another more than we can fathom.

When parents gather in supportive, empowering environments to share insights and validate one another's experiences and needs, this can have a huge, long-reaching impact on society as a whole. As more and more women and men make self-care a priority, our culture will shift as well, perhaps permanently, so we are all living from the inside out, rather than the outside in.

The self-care pebbles that each of us drop in the pond today will create ripples for generations to come. Recently, as I drove my son to school, I mused out loud, "Should I go to yoga or Nia this morning?" I love both, but I was juggling a full day with a lot of deadlines, so I was pondering which might support a more flowing schedule.

While we waited in line at school to reach the drop-off point, my son asked me, "Well, Mom, how do you feel after you go to yoga?" "Hmmm, wise and calm," I replied. "And how do you feel after you go to Nia?" he asked. "Alive and happy," I said, enjoying this conversation and how engaged my child was in helping me. "So," he continued, "what kind of day do you want to have — wise and calm or happy and alive?" "Oh, wise and calm!" I said, after reflecting on what I most needed that day. "Yes, it's definitely a wise and calm day."

Moment to moment we have opportunities to teach self-care by example, and to learn from our little ones as well. Learning to deeply nurture myself has helped me to relax and learn to "go with the flow": that way, the little things stay little (like my son not picking up his toys) and don't become front-page news; I have more space around my thoughts and become more present and less reactive; I'm kinder and more compassionate with others (whether it's a waitress, family member, or business partner); and I feel and connect more deeply to God as opposed to experiencing God as a concept in my head. Self-care increases my sense of interconnectedness to everyone around me.

As I continue to peel back the layers of the "self-care onion" and experience more self-compassion, greater self-acceptance, and the holy grail of self-love, I marvel at how this practice keeps evolving and what a profound impact it's had on my life.

Pat on the Back

WHAT'S WORKING?

What is one thing you're doing now — or have done in the past few months — to nurture yourself?

Putting It into Practice

MAKING SELF-CARE A PRIORITY

Set aside twenty minutes for quiet reflection. Get comfortable: put on some cozy clothes and make some hot or iced herbal tea. Have your journal nearby in case you want to elaborate on the exercise below. If the concept of self-care is new to you, take it slowly and ease into this. Answer the following questions:

- Which area of self-care — physical, mental, emotional, or spiritual — do you feel most called to focus on right now?
- What concrete steps can you take this month in this area to make self-care a priority, such as enlisting the help of your partner or a friend so you can take a solo date?
- What would motivate you to make your self-renewal a priority? Review the list under "Why Self-Care?," page 8, and list your top three reasons for practicing self-care.

Next, set up a dinner or coffee date with a friend or trusted mentor to discuss self-care and the ideas in this chapter. When you meet, take turns sharing your answers to the above questions. Then discuss the specific self-care practices and steps you will each follow over the coming month.

I recommend committing to a conscious self-care practice for a month. During that time, notice when and if the four areas of self-care — physical, mental, emotional, and spiritual — cross your radar. At the end of the month (or more often), check in with your friend and discuss how things are going. Above all, if you haven't made as much progress as you hoped, be easy on yourself. Don't forget: change happens one step at a time.

Imagine a New Way of Being
A JOURNALING EXERCISE

Close your eyes for a minute and place one hand over the center of your chest. Take a deep breath. Observe with curiosity and compassion whatever thoughts and feelings this chapter has stirred up for you. When you're ready, explore the following questions in your journal:

- What would your life look like if you were attuned and responsive to your needs?
- How would it feel to put yourself first and make your self-renewal a priority?
- How might your family relationships change if you regularly took time for self-care?

PAUSE for PEACE
Emotional Checkup

If I asked you how you were feeling right now, would you know?
Most of us are moving so fast, we have no idea how or what we're
feeling — what our emotional barometer is reading. Close your eyes,
take a few deep breaths, and place one hand over the center of your chest
and your other hand on your belly. Pause, enjoy the stillness, then check
in with the utmost compassion and some curiosity: What have you been
feeling lately? Calculate this on a scale of 1 to 10, with 1 being "I'm about
to have a nervous breakdown" and 10 being "I'm feeling blissed out."
Does your response surprise you? Often the act of checking in can be
cathartic in itself. I do this exercise often to help me tune in and see
what I need and how I'm doing. You can also do this exercise
with your family members to help them learn to tune in to
their emotional state in the moment.

Chapter 2

PEACE BEGINS with ME: A JOURNEY to WHOLENESS

During my twenties and throughout much of my thirties, my internal dialogue went like this: "Relationships are hard, and I don't really have any great models for how to be in a relationship, so I'll probably never be very successful." My parents divorced at age forty-eight after twenty-six years of marriage and seven kids together. Both sets of grandparents went through divorces, my brother divorced after fourteen years of marriage, and I've had good friends in long-term marriages that ended in divorce.

Can you relate?

A few years ago my husband and I visited Big Sur, California, to celebrate our tenth wedding anniversary. During our vacation, I realized how much I had changed in the past ten years — regarding how I view my husband, myself, and our partnership. For instance, one morning while hiking down a quiet sandy trail that led to the ocean, I asked my husband some big "life questions." He paused for a while and responded thoughtfully. Then I waited to see if he'd reciprocate and ask me the same questions.

He didn't. And I was fine. Actually, more than fine.

Ten years ago, I would have been irritated, hurt, and possibly angry for hours at his "insensitivity." I would have perceived this as a barrier to our emotional intimacy! Today, after a lot of inner exploration, I've come to understand three things that changed how I viewed this experience: First, my beloved is an introvert. His internal world is vast and rich, and he needs time and space to digest introspective questions. Second, he and I don't need to talk or discuss every topic to enjoy intimacy. Often our most intimate moments are found in silence. But most of all, I no longer need my husband to make me feel complete or whole. I know who I am. I am in touch with my needs. If something is important to me, I can bring it up and explore it with him, and he's always receptive to listening.

I felt giddy at this realization, and we finished our walk to the waves in silence. Later, I also shared this epiphany with him. Of course, at first he felt horrible for not reciprocating my questions, until I explained that I was mentioning it, not because I was upset, but only to share the important things I'd realized about myself.

UPON ARRIVAL, PROCEED to BAGGAGE CLAIM

Relationships of all types can be challenging. In particular, family members, partners, and children often develop a sixth sense for how to push our buttons. For myself, to become less reactive, I've had to slowly become more self-aware, compassionate, loving toward myself, and attuned to my needs — which has made me a much more emotionally present parent and partner.

Some of the keys are to show up in our relationships with a soft and open heart, a healthy perspective, and a full cup rather than a half-empty one. Before we can do that, however, we have to examine ourselves: we have to release and heal old self-limiting beliefs by understanding what we're holding on to and why.

We all have emotional baggage. Ever heard the phrase "the issues are in the tissues"? Our beliefs, scars, and old patterns from our family lineage, childhood, culture, education, and birth order all significantly affect our worldview and habitual ways of being. These, in turn, guide how we show up and relate to our family members.

Some days we get easily triggered. Maybe our child not putting their dirty clothes in the laundry room sends us over the edge, while other days they could break the front door and we'd just roll with it. Our state of being has the most impact on how we respond to external circumstances. Some days we receive the gift of observing when we're stuck in an old pattern or way of seeing things, and other times we just feel stuck, or else constantly critical or judgmental, thinking of our partner or children: "If they'd just listen to me, we'd all be happier!"

When this happens, look inward to see if you have any unclaimed baggage. For instance, when my son, Jonah, was about to turn ten, he and I went through a really difficult patch. He's a beautiful, passionate, mature, intense kid, and as he reached adolescence, his level of defiance at times overwhelmed me. A simple request to finish homework or put his dirty dishes in the sink could invoke an emotional tsunami. Since I have a tendency to be controlling, our interactions were a Molotov cocktail.

"Often we have to break down in order to break through."
— Renée Trudeau

After a particularly hard stretch involving lots of crying jags (mostly mine), I called Terri, a parent educator, and asked if my husband and I could see her for a session. I was exhausted from the stressful interchanges and needed help. After I explained our situation, Terri turned to me and gently shared, "You are going through mourning — Jonah is no longer a child. He's an adolescent." Terri went on to highlight some of the science around early-adolescent behavior and how best to support my son; in short, offer love and acceptance, not solutions and tips for improvement. After that illuminating session, things got much easier in our home — not yellow-brick-road happy, but the crying and yelling diminished greatly.

In part, the improvement occurred because my husband and I tweaked our language and gave Jonah more freedom, but mostly things changed because my husband and I shifted ourselves internally. We realized we were holding unrealistic, supersized fears that were causing us to be overly critical; our heads had become filled with visions of our out-of-control nine-year-old turning into a sixteen-year-old heroin addict. We were "parenting from the future" and from our own fears and wounds, rather than from the present moment, which was what our son most needed. This aha moment and shift in our awareness are what created the big shift in our family dynamic that we needed. Often we have to break down in order to break through.

HEALING IS a PROCESS, NOT an EVENT

My dad's favorite song growing up — which he'd sing loudly, much to our embarrassment, when we attended Mass or when he was out working in the yard — was "Let There Be Peace on Earth." The song continues "...and let it begin with me."

As I look back at my upbringing and the many spiritual traditions we were introduced to, it's clear my parents strove to realize this. They were doing their best to contribute to a peaceful community by working to create peace within their own hearts through practices such as meditation and prayer. I believe that, more than anything, they desired to teach us how to seek out and find this peace within ourselves. I watched them struggle with their emotional wounds, with little support and without taking time for themselves, while juggling the demands of parenting seven kids. *Peace* was not the word that defined our household, and yet I have never forgotten my parents' persistent efforts to create peace. Healing is an ongoing process that continues, in some form or fashion, throughout our entire lives.

One Saturday, I led a self-renewal workshop for moms at a teen girls' conference. We were exploring self-care and identifying doorways for self-nurturing and nourishment, and at the end of our session, I gave each woman a juicy clementine orange. I invited them to close their eyes and "fill" the orange with whatever they most needed in that moment — emotional support, the ability to say no, self-acceptance, courage, clear boundaries, and so on. After this reflective meditation, I asked them to slowly smell, peel, and mindfully eat their orange — which now symbolized the act of fully "receiving" the qualities they had just imbued it with.

After the exercise, the moms — who were mostly single, working women juggling way too many obligations — shared how difficult it was to slow down and become present and attuned to their needs. Christy, whose son has Down syndrome, said, "It felt foreign and kind of scary. I just never take time to get in touch with what's going on inside of me." Marion, a single mom to three teenagers, confessed she was afraid to slow down because she was worried that if she allowed herself to "feel her feelings," she might never recover or be able to return to her typical zero-to-ninety pace. Can't we all relate to this at one time or another?

When the workshop ended, almost all the women asked for extra oranges to bring home to their teenage daughters, so they could repeat the exercise with them. I happily obliged.

AN EXPLORATION: HEALING from the INSIDE OUT

What do you need to heal? In the following journaling exercise, write responses to the following questions, and give yourself permission to really tap into what you need. Find a comfortable, cozy space and make sure you have at least an hour of uninterrupted quiet time. If you have a history of emotional or physical abuse, be extra gentle with yourself. If a question stumps you or causes you too much discomfort, skip it and come back to it later or disregard it completely. Then, take time afterward to share your responses with a trusted friend, mentor, family member, or therapist.

- What issue or relationship do I most need to focus on healing right now? Consider writing (but not sending) a letter to your mom or dad about your childhood: What would you most want them to know? How would it feel to write your parents a letter of forgiveness for their shortcomings?
- What did I need to get from my family that I never received? How can I give that to myself now?
- Have I talked to my siblings about our family growing up? What insight might they be able to offer about our family dynamic?
- Who are possible mentors, therapists, or ministers I can go to for a heart-to-heart? Who in my life allows me to be vulnerable and show up "warts and all"?

- If I could tell my parents about my family and what's important to me, what would I most want them to know?
- What do I most need from my family members that is essential to my emotional well-being?
- Am I ready to do the work to heal? Do I believe I deserve to have a joyful, connected family experience?
- What am I ready to release that's no longer serving me?
- What old wounds or blocks are keeping me from being the parent and partner I desire to be? What feelings am I not allowing myself to fully feel?
- What action am I being guided to take right now to begin my healing journey?

As you write, periodically take some deep breaths and make sure you are fully present in your body. To help find emotional balance, I highly recommend learning the Emotional Freedom Technique (www.eftuniverse.com), a wonderful acupressure-based tool for calming the emotions, which we use often in our home. One simple method is to vigorously tap your thymus gland — which supports rebalancing and stress reduction — located in the center of our chest.

Through this process of self-inquiry, we become more self-aware and develop a deeper understanding of why we do what we do. Then, as our inner state shifts and expands, our outer world begins to look different — often becoming a reflection of the healing work we've done.

Are you ready to unzip the old, bulky space suit you're wearing and fully step into a new way of being? Are you open to releasing the antiquated patterns, habits, thoughts, and ways of seeing things that no longer serve you? This is healing from the inside out.

Years ago I attended a mindfulness retreat at Kripalu Center for Yoga & Health where I was challenged to explore my old thinking, particularly about relationships. I was feeling restless and disconnected from my partner, and if asked, I could instantly come up with a nice list of things my husband "needed" to do better to enhance our emotional intimacy! On the first day of the retreat, I was paired with Elena, a French Canadian woman who was contemplating divorce. Together, we spent the better part of three days challenging our beliefs about our relationships.

On the last day, a veil lifted. While lounging with Elena on the lawn outside the retreat center, I had an epiphany: What if I was in the ideal relationship — actually my dream relationship? What if my partner was completely available for the level of emotional intimacy that I desired, but because of my stories — my clunky, outdated thinking and my own clouded lens — I just wasn't able to see what was there all along? The door to his heart opened every time I was near, but my criticisms and judgments about how things "should be" slammed it shut before we even had a chance to connect on a deeper level.

My return from that retreat marked the beginning of a major shift in how my husband and I related. I began to question the stories I had created and how I view — and show up in — all my key relationships. Healing from the inside out is an evolutionary process.

FAMILY: AN INCUBATOR for PERSONAL GROWTH

I am nineteen years old and a sophomore in college. I am home and having lunch with my dad at a local cafeteria. My parents have separated after twenty-six years together. They are on the rocks and headed toward divorce. Feeling wounded and working on his own healing, my dad is doing all he can to keep his head above water.

However, I plead with him to give my mom a break and take the kids for a while. Five of my siblings, from age five to sixteen, are still at home, and I don't think she has it in her to care for them. I have been having nightmares about my siblings floating in outer space alone. In one recurring dream, I am on my hands and knees combing through a green shag rug for small penny-sized plastic babies that have been placed in my care, but I am unable to locate them.

Yet my dad is in no place to take my siblings, and two years later — after tremendous emotional turbulence and a custody battle — my parents divorce. Afterward, my siblings only see my dad on the weekends.

Those years leading up to and immediately following my parents' divorce were some of the rockiest our family ever experienced. It was a time of intense learning and growth for me, and in hindsight, as difficult and painful as it was, it provided a truly perfect training ground for the work I'm doing now. These events held meaning and purpose that I couldn't see or appreciate at the time.

Family is sacred. It's a spiritual entity. Some believe, before we are born, we choose our families and actually enter into a sacred agreement to be

together. I used to get so mad at my mom when I was young. As a rebellious teen, I'd yell at her, "I hate you. You're so mean. I wish I was in another family." She'd always respond, "Well, your soul chose to come to us!" This always just irritated me more.

What do I believe today? Families are definitely much more than a bunch of people who happen to live together. I believe there is a divine orchestration at play. We're together for a reason. These souls. At this time. In this place. There's no more perfect incubator or hothouse for personal and spiritual growth than one's family.

Our family provides us with many opportunities, such as

- giving and receiving love, including self-love, love for others, and Divine love;
- learning compassion, empathy, and sympathy;
- heightening self-awareness by serving as one another's mirrors, and sometimes flashlights;
- experiencing deep purpose and meaning and exploring what we're really here to do;
- remembering who we really are; and
- experiencing a playground for working through our own issues.

We can't escape our family. Despite how staggeringly scary it may be, the bonds of family endure permanently. As adults, many of us understandably want to run away from our birth family and create new families through friendships and other support systems, but as my brother Kert always says, "If you think you're enlightened, go home for Thanksgiving."

But being in a family also provides us with a chance for healing — for experiencing more love, deepening our capacity to love, and choosing moment to moment to come from love.

CHOOSING LOVE over FEAR

As most great spiritual teachers tell us, we only ever have two choices in how we approach our lives and day-to-day interactions: from fear or from love.

When we come from our hearts, and family relationships are viewed through the eyes of love, we

- trust — and allow those we love to follow their unique path (even if we don't agree);
- practice acceptance and let go (of homework struggles, of who's right, and so on);
- listen from our hearts in our interactions and respond in the moment;
- communicate openly and are more receptive and flexible;
- come from a prosperity mindset and see that there is always "enough" time, attention, space, and resources;
- see everyone's true essence, who they really are, not how they're acting in the moment; and
- slow down and experience gratitude for all that happens.

When family relationships are viewed through the eyes of fear, we

- try to control, manipulate, and micromanage people and situations, thinking we always know best;
- think things are good only when they're going "our" way;
- operate from our heads all the time — overthinking and over-managing;
- become reactive and get easily triggered;

- react negatively and see problems first, instead of acknowledging what's good;
- come from a poverty mindset and feel like there is never enough; and
- punish, judge, and close ourselves off from others.

Reading these lists, who wouldn't want to choose love over fear? We prefer to expand and open rather than contracting, shutting ourselves off from one another and from feeling good. Learning to do so, however, involves cultivating awareness and consciously choosing to come from love moment to moment. This takes time and, for most of us, lots of practice.

Recently, I was challenged to step outside my own habitual reactive behavior. My husband asked me to coach him as he prepared for his upcoming performance review. This is something I used to get paid big bucks to do, so I helped him create a document outlining his accomplishments and major contributions, which he would submit to his boss before their meeting. Then, one night while we were brushing our teeth before bed, he casually mentioned that he had gotten the date wrong and missed the deadline for submitting support materials for his review. My jaw dropped, and an army of accusatory thoughts lined up in my mind; I barely managed to stop myself from unleashing a rapid-fire interrogation.

Then the next day I experienced a series of stressful setbacks — a schedule glitch, a miscommunication, a technical malfunction, a lost check, a plan that fell to pieces — and suddenly everything felt like it was going from bad to worse. I was trying to wrap up an intense week filled with lots of deadlines before leaving town on a family beach vacation, yet my swirling negative thoughts were preparing to morph from a small dust devil into a powerful full-scale tornado that would ruin the family getaway for everyone.

But something surprising happened. After stewing for a few minutes on all that had gone wrong, I paused, which has been one of the many benefits I've received from a regular morning meditation practice. Within that pause, I recognized this familiar emotional terrain — how my body was now constricting and tightening. I asked myself, "Do you really want to succumb to this downward spiral of negative thoughts? Is this *really* where you want to go and who you want to be?" Of course, it wasn't. I wanted to be open, loving, and compassionate. What I really wanted was to just let go of all my negative reactions. And so I did.

Actor Larry Eisenberg reminds us, "For peace of mind, resign as general manager of the universe."

Not every situation ends this successfully. Sometimes the allure of a good argument takes me down an old worn path. But increasingly, I'm learning to pause, check in with myself, and make sure I like the destination this particular train is headed. If I don't, I wave it on, let it keep going, and consciously choose to return to my river of well-being within.

A SHIFT in PERSPECTIVE

My first therapist used to constantly remind me, "Don't believe everything you think."

Author and spiritual teacher Byron Katie tells a great story in her book *Loving What Is* about an experience she had at a busy airport restroom. She waited in line, and finally a woman emerged from the stall nearest where she was standing. Katie walked in and was immediately irritated to see the seat was completely wet! How inconsiderate and thoughtless of that woman, she said to herself. After Katie cleaned up the seat and was done, she flushed the toilet, but as she unhooked the latch to leave, she noticed water from the commode had backfired and completely sprayed the entire toilet seat!

Katie likes to say, "We're not always wrong, only 99 percent of the time."

How often do we charge down a trail of thought based on an assumption we're clinging to — about another person, a situation, or whatever has triggered us — which in all likelihood is just flat-out not true? Perhaps the primary faulty assumption is that our problems are caused by other people or circumstances.

One fall, my son and I kept butting heads; it seemed we couldn't agree on anything. One afternoon at a yoga class, a lightbulb went off. In my family, we were raised to believe that one of the ways we expressed love was to offer solutions, ideas, and tips for how things could be "better." I realized that I was unconsciously doing this to my sweet, big-hearted son — more often than I cared to admit. I saw clearly that all he wanted from me was absolute love and acceptance. That's it. Unplugging from this piece of my personality was a huge gift, and it immediately shifted my relationship with my child and brought us back to home base. This came from my willingness to challenge my own thinking.

As a career coach, for years I heard stories from clients who felt "wronged" by bosses, coworkers, clients, companies, HR departments, and on and on. Many times, when I suggested another way of looking at a difficult situation (such as, the layoff was not personal; it was simply a necessary restructuring), they realized how skewed — and often wounded — their perception was about what had actually transpired. We're all guilty of this.

Sometimes we can get so locked into one viewpoint, we can miss out on beautiful opportunities and new ways of seeing. One Saturday morning when my son was six, we decided to let Dad sleep in while we headed out for a bike ride. For the first time, we rode to a local Mexican restaurant two miles away for potato-and-egg tacos. From my perspective, the journey was a harried obstacle course — navigating around dogs, other bikers, sprinklers, traffic lights, and cars blocking driveways, while monitoring my son's progress and safety. When we were done, I was exhausted and doubtful I'd ever suggest doing something like this again. But my little guy perceived the morning as absolute perfection: "Mom, I loved the breeze. I loved riding our bikes somewhere new. We saw so many cool things, *and* I just found a beautiful acorn on the sidewalk. This was the best morning ever!"

I'm grateful for my small, wise teacher. My son was on a completely different bike ride, and he helped me realize that a change in perspective — and how we feel — really is only a thought away.

TAKE a STAND — OWN YOUR POWER

Are you more afraid of wild success or dismal failure?

Part of the healing journey — for both men and women — involves learning to fully own your power. This means being willing to be seen and to step into the highest expression of who you are — as a person, a partner, a parent, and a spiritual being! It also means to stop playing small. Most of us rarely feel comfortable shining brightly, or letting others see our brilliance, our gifts, and our unique talents. Why is this?

I once spoke to a group of three hundred ten- to thirteen-year-old girls at a young women's career conference. As I was waiting to go on stage, I overheard a small group of four talking about their day. One of the girls was really on fire after learning about civil engineering, and she was inspired to share her career dreams with the others. I could see her face quickly shift from a state of open excitement and joy to one of embarrassment and withdrawal as the other girls subtly expressed their discomfort at seeing their young friend so clearly own and express her personal power. If only Self-Love 101 was a required course for all junior high girls.

Personal power is about living your truth, aligning with your life purpose, and expressing your authentic self. It's fully expressing your potential. Often we dance around our power, jump in and out of our power, or maybe dip a toe in our power pool — occasionally experiencing a moment of enlightenment but then retreating again to the safety of obscurity.

> *"I have to center myself each and every day or I throw everyone else off — harmony starts with me."*
> — Sasha, 35, single mother of one

After years of coaching clients, I agree with author Marianne Williamson, who wrote in her book *A Return to Love*, "It is our light, not our darkness, that most frightens us." I've found that when people feel held back in their lives and careers, it is most often due to their own insecurities, inadequacies, or fears of how others will perceive them. People often worry that if they speak their minds or score big accomplishments, their friends will say, "Who do they think they are?" People often fear that if they break away from the pack, they will be ostracized and not allowed back. So they stay safe, play small, and never really tap into or express their full potential — their personal power, as I like to call it.

When you begin to access and own your power, you align with your life purpose and authentic self. You become more whole, and you express all that you were meant to be.

Standing in your personal power takes time, practice, and courage. Here are some ways to do so:

- FIND YOUR VOICE. When you have a unique perspective or disagree with someone, do you remain quiet? Speak your mind and express how you really feel.
- MAKE SELF-CARE A PRIORITY. This is one of the best ways to send a message to yourself that you are worthy. Nurture yourself physically, emotionally, mentally, and spiritually.
- STOP CARING WHAT OTHERS THINK. You'll be working on this your whole life. Imagine who you would be or what you would do if you didn't care what others thought of you!
- BE DIRECT AND ASSERTIVE IN YOUR COMMUNICATION WITH OTHERS. Notice how people respond to the way you communicate. Sometimes we undermine our message by the way we speak. Make sure when you talk, you're heard.
- BREAK AWAY FROM THE PACK. If you'd rather go for a hike than go see a movie — listen to your needs. Don't just go along with what everyone else wants.
- LET YOUR LIGHT SHINE. Don't hold back. Let others see your talents and gifts.
- BE A FEARLESS MONEY MANAGER. It is empowering and liberating to become financially savvy — creating your own nest egg, managing a household or business budget, and getting a handle on the green stuff.
- STOP SETTLING. What do you really, really want? Stop settling. The more comfortable you become owning your power, the easier it becomes to connect to your needs and desires.
- BECOME COMFORTABLE USING YOUR MASCULINE AND FEMININE STRENGTHS. Living powerfully comes from the ability to balance both our yin and yang energies — being assertive and receptive, driving for results and letting things unfold, and so on. Learning to balance these polarities, which we all possess, can be life changing.

EMBRACING YOUR FEMININE ESSENCE

Ever heard the saying "When Mama's not happy, nobody's happy"?

A mom's ability to feel whole, alive, creative, and in touch with her feminine essence or power plays a huge role in her family's overall emotional well-being. Of course, it's important that both parents be in equilibrium. Parents often divide and conquer, each balancing the other within the family but becoming out of balance within themselves. One may be the emotional anchor, while the other is the disciplinarian; one may rule the kitchen and the other the bank account; and so on. Yet for mamas (and papas) to be truly happy, they need to be whole, healthy, and living in harmony on all levels — thinking and feeling, being and doing, giving and receiving. This helps the entire family come into equilibrium. (I discuss the yin/yang dance of balance further in chapter 8.)

I heard an interview with a relationship expert who was coaching a frustrated couple struggling to come into balance. The woman was exhausted from feeling like a drill sergeant — and she was angry that everyone in the family seemed to turn to her for their strength. The relationship coach suggested some strategies and emphasized that women are not robots or taskmasters (though we often feel that way). We are vibrant, juicy, creative, sensual beings, and if we're out of balance or not in touch with our feminine essence or power, the whole family will feel off-kilter.

Do you ever feel more like a police captain than a goddess?

Women can be imbalanced in all sorts of ways, but for many, learning to embrace our feminine essence can feel particularly challenging if we're used to carrying a heavy load and are overburdened with responsibility. (For discussions of sacred masculinity, I highly recommend the work of David Deida and Richard Rohr.) For some women, learning to embrace their feminine essence might be a critical piece of their healing work; it certainly has been for me. For years I was solely career focused. Throughout my twenties and thirties I was more interested in building my career than nurturing my femininity (I never realized I could do both). After I had my son and launched my first business, I tapped my deep well of creativity and began to actively celebrate and embrace my feminine essence and its many gifts. This awakening — that I could be both strong and soft — became pivotal to my healing on all levels.

Here are some ways I have learned to connect to my feminine essence and bring more balance and joy into family life:

- by reclaiming dance and encouraging my family to dance and move for the pure fun of it;
- by embracing pleasure and creating a pleasure-infused life at home and at work (whether that's enjoying self-massage, a lavender-infused bubble bath, or fresh flowers on my desk);
- by creating a home sanctuary, using candles, aromatherapy, family pictures, color, relaxing music, and more;
- by encouraging creative expression — whether through cooking, gardening, or building — in each member of our family and as a family;
- by embracing the natural world, both by getting into nature as a family and bringing nature into our home, such as by putting a juice glass filled with sprigs of rosemary from our yard on the dinner table;
- by practicing receptivity and allowing others to help me, so that I receive as much as I give; and
- by learning when to initiate and when to allow, rather than habitually launching into action or "fix-it" mode.

HEALING IS NOT OPTIONAL

What would happen if you continued with "business as usual" and chose not to do any healing work? Would your family keep setting you off and triggering the same issues over and over again? You bet!

As long as we continue to think and do the same things — and remain unconscious of our behavior, habitual thinking, and issues — we'll keep getting triggered. We'll experience the same reactions every time and continue to suffer and swim in our cesspool of negative habitual thought.

For two days I had the flu and felt awful. When my normally thoughtful son came home from school, he got mad at me that he couldn't watch TV. Then he was angry that he couldn't go to a friend's house until he had put away his lunch box, practiced piano, and finished his homework (his normal afternoon routine). Then when I asked him to get a box of tissues for me from upstairs, he huffed off, muttering under his breath, and slammed the pantry door.

I could feel my thinking spiraling downward as I formulated a mental list of "reasons why he should help me." We'll always have things happen that are contrary to what we want. This is a given. The question is: Will we allow ourselves to keep getting triggered every time, or will we choose a different response?

Until we change — from the inside out — how we respond to family members and interactions that cause us pain, we'll keep getting the same result and experiencing the same feelings, over and over. I think we all know this, but doing it is harder. Whenever my girlfriends and I get angry at our partners and joke about "greener pastures," we remind each other that in truth you "pick your partner and do-si-do." That is, it doesn't matter who you're with; it's always "same stuff, different day" until you begin to heal and examine your own stories and state of being.

As we slow down, pause, inquire, do the work that's needed to heal, and invite our wise selves to have a voice, we begin to experience more space around our problems and how we see things. We create breathing room in which we can choose how and when we respond to the screaming toddler, the teenager who just broke curfew, or the partner who seems constantly distracted.

As we begin to heal our inner world and come into greater wholeness, our outer world changes, too. Our choices and circumstances shift and align with our values, so we live with greater integrity with who we really are. Our outer world begins to mirror our inner world. For instance, I recently explored the difference between how I used to experience pleasure compared with what I now seek out and enjoy. Here are some of the things I used to do to experience happiness:

- Eat out, especially big, fancy meals — the richer, the better.
- Go shopping; America's favorite pastime was fun no matter how much I spent or what I bought.

- Have regular over-the-top sensory experiences, like attending large music festivals, art shows, and multisensory events drawing big crowds.
- Be outdoors and go for a hike, but only when accompanied by a food- or drink-centered soiree.
- Pack my schedule with lots of activity, stimulation, and things to see and places to go!
- Maintain a large circle of interesting, diverse friends and schedule lots of "play dates."

Here are the things I prefer to do now:

- Cook for a small group of friends and family and enjoy fresh, delicious, in-season fruits and veggies (which are even better if I get to harvest them locally!).
- Spend time relaxing with my family — playing games, swimming, or just hanging out in the backyard.
- Ensure each weekend includes long, quiet expanses of unscheduled time, which feels luxurious!
- Experience nature as much as possible in all sorts of ways: on vigorous hikes in national parks, lazy walks around the lake, and overnight trips to the mountains.
- Create space for heartfelt conversations with close friends and family — but most importantly, being with friends who let me show up "warts and all"!
- Exercise daily and in truly pleasurable ways: through yoga, dance, hikes, walks with friends, canoeing, or anything that's fun.

Just to be clear, I'm not being critical of my old ways. I still enjoy the things in the first list on occasion, but now only in moderation. By reading this book you have already started your own healing process, which is unique for each of us. You have different needs and will follow a different path than anyone else. Here are a few ideas (some of which I've mentioned already) to consider to support you on your healing journey, but first and most important — tune in and hear what would best serve you and your current life stage:

STEPS TO WHOLENESS

- Ask yourself every morning when you get up: What do I need to heal today?
- Cultivate mindfulness, the ability to live in the now, and learn to "feel your feelings."
- Write a letter of forgiveness to yourself or others (you don't have to mail it!).
- Practice daily meditation or prayer whether alone or in a community. A daily meditation and breathwork practice have had a huge impact on my healing.
- To dislodge old, stuck patterns, try some really good therapy or counseling, or if addictive behavior is an issue, tap into a twelve-step program, like Al-Anon, Debtors Anonymous, or a similar support group.
- Learn the art of surrendering and letting go.
- Explore conscious movement (like yoga, qi gong, or Nia) and breathwork.
- Join a women's or men's healing support group.
- Consciously practice self-compassion and loving-kindness.

Remember, healing is a journey, not a destination. Move slowly and give yourself lots of breathing room.

My brother Kert's therapist once said that healing work is like diving. Some of us start just by trying on a mask, some go snorkeling right away, but none of us go deep-sea diving until we're fully suited up and prepared — emotionally and spiritually. The time for this will be revealed to us when we're good and ready.

HEALING as SPIRITUAL PRACTICE

Part of our healing work can include shifting to view family life as a spiritual practice.

It changes everything if we see our family as a sacred gathering of particular souls. As I've said, I believe all families consciously choose to come together, but that doesn't mean it's easy street. The people you love and care about the most will also challenge you the most. Being in intense, intimate relationships with people will be hard at times, especially if you need a lot of time alone. (My mom was an artistic, musical, introverted, only child — and she had seven kids. Can you imagine?!) Real intimacy takes a willingness to be both vulnerable and courageous.

"Letting each family member feel their feelings and experience the full emotional range — from glee to anger — fosters a sense of resilience and trust in the strength of our relationships."
— Dawna, 50, mother of two

As a parent, I try to see my son as a wise, mature soul who just happens to be in a kid's body. I try to cultivate compassion for what that must feel like for him. That doesn't mean I treat him like an adult and let him do whatever he wants, but this perspective can help elevate and shift how we relate to each other. It helps me remember to approach my family as my greatest source of joy and the people I most want to be with.

Envision unzipping an old, outdated, cumbersome zoot suit and stepping into a lighter, freer, more enlightened version of yourself. What would this look like, and how would your relationships change? Consider the following as you look at relating to your family in a new way:

- What could I do to feel more connected to my family?
- How could I express my love to my family in new ways?
- What do I most want from my family members?
- What is my highest vision for my family? How do I see my partner and me interacting when our kids are grown?
- If I were to describe my family with three adjectives, what would they be?
- What do I do to enhance our family's sense of harmony and equilibrium?
- What do I do (perhaps unconsciously) to derail our sense of well-being?

- When I feel whole, alive, and emotionally fed, how does this affect my parenting?

Author Richard Carlson says, when you focus on your own healing, "something wonderful begins to happen with the simple realization that life, like an automobile, is driven from the inside out, not the other way around. As you focus more on becoming more peaceful with where you are, rather than focusing on where you would rather be, you begin to find peace right now, in the present. Then, as you move around, try new things, and meet new people, you carry that sense of inner peace with you. It's absolutely true that, 'Wherever you go, there you are.'"

As I watch my five parentless siblings hit major life milestones — marriages, divorces, new babies, moves, career changes — and observe their individual journeys toward emotional health and well-being, it makes me reflect on what I needed and wished I could have heard when I was their age.

If I was sitting across from her now, here is what I would say to my sweet thirty-year-old self:

Dearest Renée:

Your work is to remember who you *really* are. Who you are is not defined by your family history or the pains or tragedies you experienced growing up. Your parents loved in the best way they could. Moving into compassion for them can bring you to a place of liberation.

Self-awareness and self-acceptance are the doors to freedom and peace. Don't be afraid to become very acquainted with your fears, dreams, personality, self-limiting beliefs, strengths, shadow, and brilliance. Love *all* of who you are. Your ordinary self is enough — you don't need to do or be more for anyone.

Reach out and ask for help. There is never any reason to go it alone. We were designed to be interdependent. Cultivating this ability is key to your emotional health.

Release "shoulds" and become comfortable saying no with grace and ease. And watch the universe respond with delight in delivering to you what you *really* want, not what the media or society dictates you *should* want!

Allow yourself to be vulnerable and let people see your fragility as well as your strength. Sharing this side of yourself is transformative and freeing. Lastly, don't be afraid of becoming very still. You already have *all* the answers within you. You just have to get quiet enough to hear them.

With the deepest love and compassion,

Your Wise Self

If your Wise Self wrote a similar letter to your younger self, what would it say? A big part of my journey to balance and peace has been learning to cultivate a deep sense of self-compassion and know I'm doing the best I can, wherever I am on my journey.

When I lead weekend women's renewal retreats at Esalen Institute and Kripalu Center for Yoga & Health — two beautiful, world-renowned retreat centers — we set two chairs facing each other in a quiet corner of the room. Between the easy chairs is a side table with two inviting tea mugs and sometimes a lit candle. These two empty chairs serve as a symbolic invitation and reminder that the retreat is an opportunity for each woman to sit quietly and receive guidance from her Wise Self. Whether this represents God, your intuition, or a higher power, it is that which holds the highest and best for you, never leaves, and is with you always, waiting and ready to respond.

As we become more integrated and whole, we spend more time with our Wise Self. As we align with our inner knowingness and act from this place, we tap into our river of well-being, and those around us feel this and respond as well. Relationships change. Parenting shifts. Households become more harmonious. Problems evolve, become irrelevant, or disappear.

We all want to be heard, to know we matter, to feel connection and intimacy, and to feel loved and supported exactly the way we are — both parents and kids alike. So how do we get there? By starting with the utmost compassion for self, by acknowledging there is work to do (inner and outer), by having the courage to ask for and receive help, and by taking small steps.

And finally, by remembering we're not trying to "fix ourselves" but to come into the highest expression of who we are. Our true selves.

Pat on the Back

WHAT'S WORKING?

What is one thing you're currently doing — or have done in the past — to facilitate your healing and coming into greater wholeness?

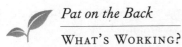

Putting It into Practice

CREATE A HEALING COCOON

Set aside twenty minutes for some quiet time. In your journal or a notebook, list all of the people, places, teachers, and things that soothe and heal you — that remind you of your innate wholeness and health. This could be a mentor or counselor, a specific yoga instructor or music teacher, certain music or songs, a place in nature or in your home, or a book or inspirational teaching. We often forget what heals us until we really pause and reflect. After you've made your list of the things that promote healing for you, take a large, blank sheet of white paper and draw a healing cocoon with yourself in the middle — surrounded by all those people, places, and things that help bring you to the highest and brightest expression of who you are. Put the picture of your healing cocoon somewhere you'll see it — maybe the bathroom, the kitchen, or your office. Remember, your job is to tap these resources when you feel stuck and need to soothe your soul and quiet your mind. This exercise may also serve to illuminate what and where your greatest areas of need are. Either way, it's all good.

Imagine a New Way of Being

A JOURNALING EXERCISE

Close your eyes for a minute and place one hand over the center of your chest. Take a deep breath. Observe with curiosity and compassion whatever thoughts and feelings this chapter has stirred up for you. When you're ready, explore the following:

- What might your life look like as you heal your unresolved issues and relationships?

- How does it feel when you experience true emotional well-being and resiliency, and you don't take things personally?
- How might your family's sense of peace and harmony shift as you heal and come into greater wholeness?

Part II

RECONNECT

PAUSE for PEACE
An Intentional Beginning

Start your day in a new way. First thing in the morning, do you habitually turn on the TV or the radio, or check email? Instead, at least once try easing into your day unplugged, and if you can, make it a new habit. Upon waking, or at some point in your morning routine, take a few minutes to stop, close your eyes, tune in, and listen to what you most need. Try some gentle stretching, a few minutes of stillness and meditation, a short brisk walk around the block, or perhaps journaling for five minutes in your car before you walk into work. Meditation teachers say spending as little as five minutes to mindfully and intentionally enter each day can have a huge impact on our overall well-being.

Chapter 3

PEOPLE FIRST, THINGS SECOND: THE DIGITAL DIVIDE

How do you feel about technology? Do you love it and adopt every new device, or is your only phone still attached to the wall and you have to get up to change the TV channels? More importantly, what effect has technology and the Internet had on your family and its sense of togetherness? Is technology bringing your family closer together or driving you farther apart? Like most, you probably feel a deep ambivalence, swinging between feeling like a master of and a slave to your own technological devices.

When I surveyed families around the United States and Canada on what derails their sense of emotional well-being, overuse and misuse of technology was the number one saboteur to familial harmony. Surprised? I think as a society we're all a bit shocked by how quickly these relatively new tools have infiltrated every part of our lives. We see the transformation all around us. One sunny afternoon while enjoying the spring breeze and sitting on a blanket at a local park, I was amazed to realize virtually everyone over the age of five had a device in their hands. One father was walking purposefully, his eyes glued to his smart phone, while his three-year-old son ran along-side him, struggling to keep up and trying to get his attention to show him some snails he'd found. The father never paused, saying, "Not now, Ethan, Daddy's busy."

Meanwhile, on the playground, three moms gathered around the play-scape with their heads bowed over their small rectangular devices, their young toddlers playing on their own nearby. On a weathered bench, two tweens sat side by side, ignoring each other but not their electronic thumb toys. If a troupe of aliens suddenly landed on the playground, what would they have thought? Were humans simply devoted to the wisdom contained in their palm-held appliances above and beyond all else, or were these electronic devices literally connected to their bodies — like appendages — and that was why no one could put them down?

USE the POWER BUTTON

Last summer my friend Diane and I took our kids to her community pool. After the kids were slathered in sunscreen and splashing in the water, we sat on the edge of the pool, our feet dangling in the water. Diane commented, "Our summer has been really great. It's amazing how different our lives have been since we cut out TV. We're spending more time together as a family. We're outdoors more, we listen to music in the evening, and everyone seems a lot happier, less irritable, and more enjoyable to be around."

I admit I was somewhat shocked that someone could cut out TV entirely, since TV-time negotiations are a recurring battle for most families, including mine. Diane admitted, "After we moved into our new home, we just never got around to having the cable turned on. For weeks, the kids asked when it would be fixed. I told them I hadn't had a chance to schedule the cable guy. Eventually, we all forgot about it. At the beginning of our TV fast, my son Aaron said, 'Mom, not having the TV is like losing a member of the family!' When I heard this, it really struck me how habitual it had become for us to always have it on. Scheduling the cable guy ended up being the best thing I could have ever dropped off my to-do list!"

Every family I know navigates the technology two-step, that devilish dance over the power switch, screen time, and whether to buy the next electronic device du jour. If you feel like your family is suffering from overuse or abuse of technology, it's important to hit the pause button and reassess how you're using these tools. Any negative impact on your relationships is a problem. Even if you think the issue doesn't affect you, it's still useful to get a clear picture of how much time you spend on your devices and the impacts they are having. Ultimately, you want decisions about how and when your family interacts with technology to reflect your family's priorities and values. To begin, take the following informal "family media use" survey:

> *"Is technology bringing your family closer together or driving you farther apart?"*
> — Renée Trudeau

- What electronic devices are you currently using and who uses them? List every device in your household and the users for each.
- How often do you and your kids use each device? List the number of hours and days per week for each user and device. Add up how much each family member spends on "screen time": Does this match your impression?
- As a couple, have you and your partner discussed media use and your children? Have you agreed on what age and standards are appropriate, now and in the future? How do you determine if media is age appropriate — do you have a resource to help you (such as www.commonsensemedia.org)?
- As a parent, have you established any media-use guidelines with your children? What are they, and do they address all the devices you own?
- Overall, do you feel there is a problem with overuse or does the usage seem appropriate? Are there certain devices or situations that are more problematic than others?
- Assess both the specific ways technology helps your family, as a source of enjoyment and togetherness, and how it gets in the way of togetherness, communication, and well-being.

Many parents find that just taking time to reflect on and answer these questions can serve as a real wake-up call. Sometimes it can be easy to forget that we choose how and when to interact with technology; we are not in control if we allow it to interfere with family time. Explore this topic consciously, compassionately, and with curiosity. Overuse and misuse of technology are problems that can escalate and worsen as kids get older. Most of all, it's not going away, and the issues and impacts only get more complex and serious over time.

It's worth keeping in mind some of the recent research related to screen time and electronics and how they affect children and families:

- The amount of time families spend together each week, on average, is less than five hours; people spend more time with computers than they do with their partners or children.
- When four- to seven-year-old kids were asked if they'd prefer to spend time with Dad or to watch TV, 45 percent left Dad holding the baseball and glove alone so they could fatten up on cartoons.
- Children today spend an average of six hours each day in front of the computer and TV but less than four minutes a day in unstructured outdoor play.
- Children and youth from age eight to eighteen are spending as much as sixty hours a week involved in electronic media.
- Childhood obesity is on the rise: two-thirds of American children can't pass a basic physical, and 40 percent show early signs of heart and circulation problems.
- On average, each hour of TV watched per day by preschoolers increases by 10 percent the likelihood that they will develop concentration problems and other symptoms of attention-deficit disorders by age seven.
- In 2008, people consumed three times as much information each day as they did in 1960.
- Our attention is constantly shifting; computer users at work change windows or check email or other programs nearly thirty-seven times during an hour.

- Among Americans, 33 percent say the TV is always on during dinner, while 27 percent say it's on half the time or sometimes.

Yes, communication technology has numerous benefits: national and geographic borders have collapsed, grassroots efforts are easier to mobilize, a wealth of information is at our fingertips, we can connect easily with family and friends who live far away, we can enjoy the flexibility of a "mobile" workplace, and much more. That doesn't mean there aren't also numerous downsides to carefully assess and manage.

THE EMOTIONAL PRICE of a PLUGGED-IN LIFE

For many folks, discussing the impacts of technology can be an emotionally charged topic. It's important to take it seriously and explore this topic with thoughtfulness and care. In fact, one clear impact from the overuse of technology is that it causes our stress levels to go up. We feel like we're "on" 24/7, we have trouble relaxing, we tend to overeat and become less active, and we can get overstimulated. This releases stress hormones, adrenaline, and cortisol, which negatively affect our physical well-being and ability to sleep. All these impacts make it easier to succumb to addictive behaviors. Plus, we're learning that excessive multitasking via technology negatively affects productivity, creativity, and our ability to balance left- and right-brain thinking (to name just a few consequences).

Parenting experts agree that the adverse effects of too much screen time for kids can include learning problems, concentration and attention-deficit issues, obesity, depression/anxiety, difficulty connecting with others, sexualization at a young age, more aggressive/violent behavior, and higher consumption of junk food. Further, since most of this technology is relatively new, we have yet to learn what the long-term mental, physical, and emotional health repercussions will be from excessive use or misuse of technology. In general, though, it's a simple equation: kids who spend more time on media spend less time reading, outdoors, and playing music. This is true for any of us: when we're plugged into electronics, we're not connected to each other.

Sonya, a mother to two boys ages ten and twelve, said, "I started noticing a correlation between my sons' moods and their use of electronics. The more time they spent plugged in — whether that was playing video games, listening to their iPod, or watching TV — the grumpier, more distant, and more defiant they were. It's hard to believe that screen time has such a big impact on their demeanor — and in turn, on our family mood as a whole — but it does."

> "We take time to greet and hug one another in the morning and when we see each other after school and work. We also make an effort to give each other compliments and praise, at least once a week!"
> — Sara, 43, mother of five

As my friend Joan, a child psychologist, shared, "You have to wonder: What are we missing out on when we're plugged in so much? Do we have enough time for what matters most? And if we're plugged in to this degree and 'always on,' how is it affecting our ability to be present when we're *not* online?"

WALKING the WALK

As much as we worry about the full impact of the media revolution on our culture, our families, and our kids, we also have to address a more pointed question: Are we modeling healthy media habits ourselves? We can't expect our kids to find a healthy balance with media if we, as their parents, are in full-blown disequilibrium with technology.

When we are reminded to put "people first, things second," as this chapter's title encourages, something deep within us says, "Yes!" Our heartfelt intention is always to be available to those we love no matter what. When push comes to shove, no work deadline, football game, or email is more important than our partner and children. But, like the father I saw in the park, are we truly living this, or is technology slowly undermining our values?

Here are some honest confessions from clients, colleagues, and friends:

- Joe shares that he often stays later at the office than is necessary after his workday is done so he can "escape" to the Internet for mindless surfing and Facebook posts before he heads home to the challenges of family life.

- Susan says she's slumped into a habit of texting and emailing because it's easier and takes less energy than calling or having face-to-face conversations, and she admits that her relationships are suffering because of it.

- Tim, a minister, shares that he counsels couples weekly whose trust, intimacy, connection, and ability to communicate have been corroded and even shattered due to the epidemic of Internet porn.

- Michelle, who works from home as a self-employed graphic designer, says it's far too easy to slip away from her family to handle "just one more email," and this is seriously affecting her ability to be present with her kids.

- Doug admits that when he takes his kids to the playground, he can't resist the overwhelming urge to pull out his smart phone. Often an hour of mindless email and surfing can go by, and he's so oblivious that, he says, he might as well as be on another planet.

- John says that their family dinner hour is often a crazy circus where each family member is responding to texts and emails, and none of them are present for each other.

- Jill says that her system becomes so revved up from being plugged in all the time that, when she's not online, she finds it hard to slow down, be present with her family, and return to a relaxed state of being.

Perhaps one reason we, as parents, are so worried about the effect of technology on our children is that we know firsthand what it is doing to us — how easy it is to become addicted to smart phones, Facebook, email, text messaging, video games, and the constant pull of an online world that never sleeps.

As an entrepreneur, I have been guilty of letting "urgent business emails" interrupt family time and pull me away from my loved ones, even on the weekends. At the same time, we've patterned our approach to technology after my parents': we rarely watch TV, don't have cable, and limited and postponed video game use until our son was older. As we explain to him, we've made these choices in order to make time for what's most important to us: family dates and meals, expanses of unscheduled time, reading, thoughtful conversation, music, taking walks in nature, and having cultural adventures. And honestly, after spending time together on things that nourish us, there are no more hours for anything else! These are the things that most often get displaced by the overuse of technology, and yet they are the very things that therapists, researchers, and parenting educators agree that we need for our own personal, emotional, and spiritual well-being.

We're living in chaotic times. The level and speed of change and the volume of information we manage daily are staggering. As we feel more unbalanced, many are beginning to counter this intuitively by slowing down, hitting the pause button, and examining our use of technology. Indeed, sometimes it's not until we turn off our devices that we realize exactly what we're missing. The question I keep coming back to: "How does it affect our quality of 'being-ness' with those we love when we're *not* plugged in?"

THE GIFTS of BEING UNPLUGGED

One way to balance and even counteract the effects of technological overload is to engage in regular "media fasts" — that is, going cold turkey and unplugging for an entire day, a few days, or a week, and on rare occasions for a month or longer. During a typical media fast, you might refrain from engaging in any social media, electronic communications, or entertainment, but you could work on a computer if it's a requirement of your job. I have many colleagues who have made media fasts part of their routine, and they say the experience always has a huge impact on their perspective. I have done and noticed the same thing myself. I went offline for a month to work on this book, in which my only electronic interaction was using my computer for writing — which I kept to a minimum, writing longhand instead — and responding once a week to email from my staff. I was excited about the possibilities that could come from unplugging, and the experience turned out to be a huge gift: insights and revelations were flying at me so fast, I could barely catch them all.

I noticed a range of effects from being unplugged from technology for an extended period of time:

- My body was more relaxed, my shoulders felt open, my heart rate slowed, and I didn't feel that constant adrenaline surge.
- My thinking quieted down. There were more pauses between thoughts, I experienced more spaciousness, and I was more reflective and observant.
- I was more present and less reactive in my relationships; I was a better parent, boss, partner, friend, and sister.
- I was much more creative and willing to try new things; I felt my perspective on life, work, and family expand and soften.
- I could see with ease what mattered most. When I returned to my desk afterward, the tall stack of "action items" seemed a lot less urgent than before.
- My tolerance for everyday stress went way down. I questioned some of my old habitual behaviors — such as pushing and rushing to be as productive as possible in order to feel good about myself.

Finally, and somewhat shockingly, I found that I hadn't missed anything while I was gone. Then, as I thought back on it, I realized I never have. I grew up with very little access to TV. I vaguely remember watching the occasional *Star Trek* episode, but I'm hopelessly out of the loop when it comes to most 1970s and 1980s pop culture references, and so today I usually always lose at Trivial Pursuit! That's about the only negative impact. But I never remember missing TV as a child. My siblings and I were too busy building forts, making mud dams, exploring the nearby woods, collecting locust

> *"Time spent together working on something — whether it's trying to figure out a game puzzle, hiking to a Geocache, park clean-up days, or cooking dinner — helps us to recalibrate and relax."*
> — Doug, 47, father of four

shells, painting rocks, cooking eggs on the hot sidewalk, and attempting baked Alaska in the kitchen.

MEDIA GUIDELINES, SAYING "NO," and BABY STEPS

Parenting consciously and making decisions that mirror your heart and innermost values take guts, no matter what the issue is. They require an unwavering commitment to your family's well-being, in both the short and long term, as well as weathering the disapproval of your children. As we know, it's harder to say no than to say yes — particularly when that no goes against the norm of our culture. Your kids are not likely to celebrate the establishment of media guidelines, and you may find any rules difficult to follow as well. When we're overworked and exhausted, the electronic babysitter is easy to turn to and always available. Yet as we've seen, this seemingly harmless choice can develop into a negative habit that can create an ocean of disconnection, frazzled nerves and minds, and an ongoing barrier to true intimacy.

So begin with baby steps. Invite in self-compassion. Cultivate a sense of curiosity: What would happen if I became less plugged in? How can I model this for my kids? What are some half measures and partial steps I could try? What fun things could I replace screen time with? When are the most important times when I want my family unplugged (for example, during dinner or on Sundays)?

Sit down with your partner, or with your entire family, including the kids, and discuss everyone's priorities and values — what is most important for your family? What is essential for each individual and for the entire family's emotional well-being? Make a list; this may include unscheduled time, physical activity, playing in nature, eating dinner together, not feeling rushed, making time for creative or free play, and so on.

Then, take a look at your schedule. How are you using your waking hours? Outside of work and school, how many "free" hours does each person have, and how much time does the family have together? For most families, this may amount to only three to four hours of free time together a day. Many families find that once they've identified and scheduled what's really important to them, there's not much time left for TV, Internet surfing, and video games.

Here are some of the ways families are taming the technology dragon. Perhaps one of these ideas will resonate as you develop media guidelines for your family. Give yourself the freedom to experiment, discarding what doesn't work and keeping what does:

- If you watch TV every night, try giving it up for one night a week. Then progressively add more TV-free nights each week (until you reach three or four), and instead enjoy music, reading, time outdoors, or playing games on those evenings.
- If your habit is to often or always have the TV on as background noise, replace this with a classical music station. (My family finds this to be really calming in the morning and at dinnertime.)
- Some families allow their kids to have screen time only on the weekends — establish a total number of hours (say, two to five) that your kids can spend however they like from Friday to Sunday.
- Ditch the cable and only use the TV for watching family-friendly movies, either through a subscription service or by checking DVDs out of the library. Then, make a regular occasion of "family movie night" — reserve one night of the week for watching a movie you can all talk about afterward.
- Allow for one hour of educationally oriented screen time a day, and schedule this time for when Mom and Dad need it the most, such as while cooking dinner, replying to emails, and so on.
- Maintain a land line and answering machine at home. This way you can screen phone calls without interrupting precious family time.
- Insist that all cell phones and electronics be turned off during meals and whenever the family is enjoying time together.
- For the parents: abstain from getting online before work in the morning or after work in the evenings. These are natural family-gathering and transition times each day, so make your priority being present for your kids and for each other as a couple. Talk, connect, and share the day's events.
- Consider making electronics off-limits during everyday car rides

around town. Let your child sit quietly and "get bored" looking out the window, or use travel time as an ideal moment for talking about school, friends, and what's going on in your child's life.

- Avoid temptation by *not* getting a smart phone. These gadgets are a slippery slope, and how much do you really *need* all that they do? Instead, get a regular, basic cell phone with texting (you'd be surprised how many are choosing this!).

- Move the TV from the family room, or the center of your house, to an upstairs guest room. It's interesting to see how viewing habits change, and usually lessen, when the TV is in an out-of-the-way spot.

- Make one weekend day entirely, 100 percent unplugged, with no media and no phone calls at all until a certain hour in the evening. Reserve this day for 100 percent family time, and make it fun: go hiking or to museums, make fancy all-day meals, visit friends or relatives, or go swimming. Initially, long stretches of unstructured time may seem hard to fill, but propose this as an experiment and give your family's collective creativity a chance. Your older kids might continue to complain, but I bet they will secretly like it!

"Sometimes it's not until we turn off our devices that we realize exactly what we're missing. The question I keep coming back to: 'How does it affect our quality of "being-ness" with those we love when we're not plugged in?'"
— Renée Trudeau

As parents, we need to change our own mindsets and behaviors and really take charge of the technologies in our homes. It's like eating. You need a balanced diet. You don't want to raise your kids on junk food, and you don't want their whole worlds to revolve around screen time. The earlier you create healthy habits in this arena, the better. I've found looking at our media diet and paying close attention to what types of messages, images, and themes we're consuming can be helpful.

Jana shared, "My kids and I had gotten into a habit — really a slump — of watching the same programs on TV every week. They weren't great shows; it was just 'what we did.' One night we all ended up playing soccer in the backyard instead of being glued to the screen. I was surprised at how much better we all slept that night and how much happier everyone seemed in the morning. It really got me thinking about how I want to change our habits around TV — not only when we watch it, but what we watch."

Plus, once the complaining dies down and kids accept a new routine, you may be surprised by what you find. My brother, a thirty-seven-year-old technology hound and dad of two, recently discovered his three-year-old son actually loves going to the library — just as much as he used to like playing Angry Birds on dad's smart phone. Baby steps.

In fact, all the families I've known and coached that have made a conscious decision to set up media-use guidelines, instill boundaries, and in general "consume" less media have found this has made a huge impact on their personal well-being and on their family's sense of peace and harmony.

LIFE, UNPLUGGED

After leading an out-of-state retreat, I gave myself the gift of a day off for rest, completely unplugged. No laptop, no cell phone, no email, no phone calls, no TV — I went totally offline in every way.

I started my day off walking on a beautiful nature trail that runs through the center of the city. My favorite path takes me to the quieter, less-populated area of the trail where I get to see a lot of wildlife — bats, herons, swans, ducks, squirrels, cranes. The weather was clear and sunny; it felt so good not to have to rush back to conference calls or meetings, to be completely untethered from email.

After a lunch of ripe mangos, sweet strawberries, huge creamy avocados, and brown rice California rolls from Whole Foods, I spent time in our backyard smelling herbs, listening to the birds, sitting on the rocks around our water fountain, and enjoying a lazy nap in my backyard hammock. Later, I felt inspired to cook broccoli-ginger-tofu stir-fry for my family, and then we all went for a walk in our neighborhood at dusk — seeing who could spot the first firefly.

When I returned to my office the next day, my mind was clear and focused, my creative juices were flowing, and I could see with absolute clarity what most needed my attention and time.

Our days are filled with constant demands; we must solve, manage, and coordinate all areas of our lives. Often this requires a lot of time on the computer and on email. Yet could spending one day a week "unplugged" actually make us more productive?

As you explore how to tame the technology dragon, tread slowly. Approach this potential lifestyle change with curiosity and ask "What if?" a lot. Some parents confess their kids already currently consume so much media they're afraid of the backlash if they propose a change. Kids are resilient. They want and need clear boundaries, and they want *you* in their lives more than any digital device, no matter how wonderful or educational it may seem.

Of course, no one ever died from watching too much *American Idol* or posting another Facebook status. But what would you really miss if you turned off the TV and the computer? What would living a more heart-centered life look like right now? And which would you rather have your kids remember: important dinner conversations and a sunrise hike or the latest viral video?

Pat on the Back

WHAT'S WORKING?

What is one thing you are doing right now — or have done in the past — to manage your family's media use and ensure you're not plugged in 24/7?

Putting It into Practice

UNPLUG FOR A MEDIA FAST

Ready for an adventure?! I challenge you and your family to unplug for an entire day. If this makes you nervous, schedule it for when you are least likely to want to be plugged in: during a vacation or on a holiday weekend. Pick what you anticipate will be a quiet, slow day, and step away from all your electronic devices — phones included — for a full day. Don't cheat: no computer, TV, GPS, handheld device, gaming system, or phone use (except in an emergency). As important, pay conscious attention to your own state of mind and the interactions of your family during this experiment.

During the day or afterward, record your observations in your journal or a notebook. How did a one-day media fast affect you and your family? What was hard and what was easy? What surprised you? What gifts arose from this experience? Share them with your family, and perhaps use the experience as inspiration for change.

Imagine a New Way of Being

A JOURNALING EXERCISE

Close your eyes for a minute and place one hand over the center of your chest. Take a deep breath. Observe with curiosity and compassion whatever thoughts and feelings this chapter has stirred up for you. When you're ready, explore the following:

- What would it look like for your family to consciously unplug — and to be more connected to one another? What is one step you could take right now to support this?
- How would it feel to not be so tethered to your phone, your computer, and your other electronics — what might the benefits or payoffs be?
- How might your life or relationships change if you put people first and technology second?

PAUSE for PEACE
Return to Mother Earth

As soon as you finish this paragraph, stop reading and try the following: head out to your yard (or to the closest green space) for five minutes. Find a nice spot that calls to you. If weather permits, take off your shoes and socks and feel the grass and earth under your feet. Place your hands on the bark of a tree, dip your toes in running water, pick up some fallen leaves. Close your eyes. Breathe in deeply. What do you feel...hear...smell...observe? What sensations do you feel in your body? Does being outside affect your mood or perspective? The healing power of nature is often only steps away from our work space. Remember to allow yourself to soak up this amazing, free, and always available gift.

Chapter 4

NATURE: THE ULTIMATE ANTIDEPRESSANT

One spring when my son was seven years old, he and I were hiking alone on a remote trail in Big Bend National Park in west Texas. My husband had gone back to the car to get the camera. The air was still except for the occasional sound of a hawk's wings as it circled above us and the steady crunch of our hiking boots on the uneven dirt path. We walked together in silence, holding hands.

A loud rustling in a bush up ahead grabbed our attention. We paused and exchanged mischievous smiles. Without words, we shared our excitement and reverence for this sacred place and for our love of adventure and the unknown. This vast, little-visited park is home to an abundance of wildlife — large snakes, desert rabbits, road runners, bears, and mountain lions — and in this moment, we didn't know what we might see. It felt like anything could happen, anything was possible. After a few moments of stillness, a mama javelina and her wild baby boars rumbled into view and crossed our path.

When adults reflect on their favorite childhood memories, they almost always share tales that involve the natural world: times on their uncle's farm, in a favorite tree house, in grandmother's orange grove, on family camping trips, during summer visits to the lake, or even just exploring the woods near their home. One thirty-year-old mom, Emily, once shared that her most memorable childhood experience — hands down — was the time her mom woke her up in the middle of the night with a box of donuts and a blanket to take her outside to witness a rare meteor shower that was arriving at 3 A.M. Emily said this out-of-the-ordinary experience had always stayed with her, and it instilled in her a deep appreciation for the natural world and inspired her to be adventurous and spontaneous. She says, because of her parents, she grew up experiencing and appreciating the power of nature, which made her feel more connected to herself and to the world at large.

"We make a point to schedule family dates in nature to break us away from our everyday routine: monthly camping trips to a new state park or exploring a new hiking trail together. Our children love knowing we'll be fully present with them and not distracted by phones, computers, or other adults."
— Ellen, 38, mother of two

MOTHER NATURE: A HEALING FORCE

I am eleven, and my neighbor Shannon and I sneak out of the house with my baby brother, Nathan, and an armful of baby blankets. We head to a special hilly spot near the front of our house on our two-acre, oak tree–covered property. I don't think my mom knows about our favorite game, "baby in the weeds," but we are veteran babysitters, and we treat Nathan with the utmost care. We swaddle him lovingly and then pretend to "find him" in the tall grass, reliving the story of Moses we have heard in Sunday school. We continue spinning and weaving stories — intertwining our worlds with the natural world around us: the giant bee's nest in the trees, the limestone "cave" my brothers have recently discovered and swear leads to underground tunnels, the cicadas chirping in the branches above us. We lie on our backs on the ground, playing with the baby, making grass and twig wreaths for our heads, watching ladybugs, coming up with poems, and musing about the animal-shaped clouds floating by in the sky.

Nature was an integral part of the unpredictable, adventurous journey of growing up with four brothers. Our family always had a yard — sometimes it was half an acre, sometimes fifty acres — and the three oldest kids in our family loved coming up with crazy games: goulash on the rope swing (our spaghetti-style version of bucking bronco), adventures in the abandoned woods next to our home, running tag using our zip line, Peter Pan in our tree house, scooping out honeycomb from the giant bee's nest in the live oak tree, and making intricate ant villages in the dirt.

What I remember most from these excursions and games, which were everyday occurrences, was the feeling of absolute freedom. Being immersed in nature ignited our imaginations and fed our spirits. I was an explorer — my frontier was vast, and an unlimited number of discoveries awaited me! The feeling we got from being able to explore our often uncharted natural environment — uninterrupted and with very few rules — was incomparable. Running barefoot, overturning logs to examine insect villages, making up survival games, feeling unbridled happiness upon discovering an old vintage blue medicine bottle or rusty horseshoe and imagining its origin — these were often the pinnacle of our day.

My experiences as a child were not unique, and many scientific studies and books confirm that nature is good for all of us, but particularly for kids. Time in nature is often referred to as the ultimate antidepressant because it does the following:

• It helps reduce stress and anxiety while promoting relaxation.
• It positively affects our mood and overall mental health.

- It builds our physical health and immune system through exposure to vitamin D.
- It helps us to "reset" — by restoring balance and equilibrium to our emotional and psychological systems.
- It promotes cognitive abilities, hones observational skills, and helps those with ADD/ADHD.
- It fosters problem solving and creativity at work and in school.
- It stimulates social interactions and encourages kids in relationship building and cooperative and imaginative play.
- It supports family connection and cohesiveness.

"I insist on a lot of downtime at home, so we enjoy lots of impromptu fun: wrestling, playing with the cat, digging in the mud, on-the-fly kitchen experiments, and laughing while reading comic books."
— Trisha, 46, single mother of three

Yet today, American kids spend very little time outdoors. In fact, some kids have never even been to natural areas. I live in a city, Austin, that hosts a stunning eight-mile, eight-hundred-acre greenbelt through its center — complete with streams, rock formations, cliffs, wildlife, and trails — and yet many families in our community have never visited this free treasure sitting smack in the middle of our urban life.

EXPLORING YOUR RELATIONSHIP to NATURE

What emotions surface when you think about spending time in the great outdoors? What are your favorite nature memories? Perhaps it was running in your backyard at night chasing fireflies, doing a cannonball into a cool, still lake with your dad and siblings, or sitting alone and watching birds build a nest. Or perhaps spending time in nature feels foreign to you?

In your journal, describe your relationship to nature now. As you do, consider the following questions:

- Do you love being outside and try to get outdoors with your kids every chance you get?

- Are you scared about being in some natural environments or nervous about bugs or wild animals? Mother Nature is a mighty force — it's okay if she makes you nervous. Be honest.
- Did you used to spend a lot of time outdoors prior to becoming a parent but find your life is "too busy" for nature anymore?
- Do you have young kids and are you chomping at the bit for them to get older so you can do more things with them in the great outdoors?

"Life is a mystery, not a thing to be managed. The healing power of nature recalibrates us and helps put things in perspective."
— Renée Trudeau

If chugging big tall glasses full of Mother Nature, gnats and all, leaves you feeling squeamish, then I challenge you to start with an open mind and baby steps. I went on a "nature hiatus" when I was a young adult; many times I would choose shopping, movies, and arts festivals over the great outdoors. It took me a while to return to my roots. But after I became a mom and was reintroduced to the joys of wrestling on the grass, experiencing the mood boosts I got from hours at the park on a crisp fall day, and basked in the special moments and discoveries I shared with my child in the woods, I got why this is the drug of choice for many!

START WHERE YOU ARE

If you find yourself avoiding or resisting spending more time in nature, do it anyway! Start with whatever is outside your front door. Kathy, a forty-four-year-old mom, said, "After I had my son and began to spend more and more time outdoors, I started appreciating the natural areas near our home like I never had before. My son and I feel closest when we're exploring an anthill or collecting rocks together. I'm hooked. I can't believe I forgot how powerful it is to be immersed in Mother Nature."

If it's been years since you've spent time outdoors, or perhaps you feel out of your element chasing bears and mountain lions, consider the following strategies:

NURTURING the SOUL of YOUR FAMILY

- TEAM UP. Ask your nature-loving friends for advice on local spots, and join them on their next excursion to discover hidden gems in your area.
- STAY CLOSE TO HOME. Get to know your own backyard, street, neighborhood park, and any natural areas within walking distance.
- PACK SUPPLIES. Take a glass jar and catch minnows in a nearby stream, or take a magnifying glass out to a field and see life from a bug's perspective!
- GET CAMPY. Dare yourself to go camping. This can be a wonderful experience for families; invite a group of families to join you. Take it slow and easy: sleep in "camping cabins" or set up a tent in your own backyard!
- JOIN A GROUP. Visit your local camping or outdoor store (such as REI) and sign up for a class or guided hike.
- PLAN A PICNIC. Pack a simple picnic of cold food — lunch or dinner — grab a blanket, and head to your closest park; kids love the spontaneity of picnics on a weeknight!
- MAKE IT A GAME. If hiking is no draw, play outdoor games like soccer, horseshoes, Wiffle ball, and Frisbee golf — or turn exploration into a competition: Who can spot the most squirrels, birds, or bats, or find the most unusual rocks, shells, or crystals?
- MAKE A DATE. Set up a weekly or monthly "nature date" with family and friends, and rotate which park or natural area you visit (let the kids choose!). Some families I know have dubbed these "Outdoor Adventure Clubs."
- GROW YOUR OWN GRUB. Explore container gardening and grow your own herbs and vegetables; kids love to grow their own food! Then visit a local farm (your local farmer's market is a great place to get connected to nearby farms).
- ATTUNE TO NATURE'S RHYTHMS. Consider marking the full moon, new moon, or summer solstice with a hike, outdoor drum circle, or swim — kids love ritual, and it can be a fun, meaningful way to connect to nature's rhythms.
- CREATE NEW HABITS. Make nature a daily or weekly habit. Head

to a local park after school, even if it's only one or two days a week; even a short park visit before you head home can really enhance everyone's mood!

- ENJOY EVENING STROLLS. Take evening walks in your neighborhood each night after dinner — these can be relaxing for parents and help everyone prepare for good sleep. They are wonderful, easy opportunities to observe your immediate natural environment.
- ASK THE EXPERTS. Contact your state park office and ask about their family programs. Also visit the websites for the Sierra Club (www.sierraclub.org) and the Children and Nature Network (www .childrenandnature.org) — founded by Richard Louv, author of *Last Child in the Woods* — to learn about family-oriented events in your area.
- BE ADVENTUROUS. Experience nature's "wild side" and do something you've never done before! National parks are ideal for this, since they preserve our continent's natural treasures and usually maintain accessible, family-friendly facilities. Or choose an "extreme" activity: go sea kayaking, stand-up paddle boarding, zip-lining, rock climbing, snowshoeing — anything fun. Or consider swapping homes with another family in a natural area you'd like to visit; try using a service like www.homeexchange.com.

  > *"Time spent outdoors is essential for us: hiking, swimming, boating, backyard time swinging, blowing bubbles, or flying kites. When people in our house get grumpy, we say, 'go play outside!'"*
  > — John, 37, father of two

- GET CREATIVE. Don't feel hemmed in by your urban or suburban home turf. Seek out all the green spaces you can find: botanical gardens, sculpture gardens, a rooftop garden, a neighbor's outdoor space, a school playground, or even an open plaza or square where you can watch the birds and squirrels.

Seeing the effect that being outdoors has on my family has convinced me that spending time in nature needs to be as natural and regular as breathing. For instance, one recent Saturday, nothing in our household or family was going right. Everyone seemed grumpy, disconnected, and frustrated; lack of sleep and an unbalanced diet had taken their toll. I finally suggested we surrender the day, throw some snacks and water in a backpack, and head to a wilderness preserve a short drive from our home. My husband and son begrudgingly agreed, and an hour and a half later we were laughing together, running on the trails, and feeling like all was right in the world. Nothing shifts perspective and heals like being in a beautiful natural setting! It doesn't take much. Merely getting outside at night in a place where you can see the stars — really see them in all their amazing vastness — is enough. The experience always reminds me of how small and inconsequential my worries are. Life is a mystery, not a thing to be managed. The healing power of nature recalibrates us and helps put things in perspective.

It's not a luxury to get away and immerse yourself in a natural setting. It's like oxygen. It's essential to your well-being. It's one of the greatest gifts we have available to us. In our galaxy, the sun is one of a hundred billion stars. Now how important is it to make sure you finish your laundry and your car gets washed again?

NATURE: A DOORWAY to GOD

One Sunday morning, my son and I headed down to the "church of the greenbelt," our name for one of our favorite Sunday morning nature haunts. We stopped to perch on the rocks above a gently running stream and sat quietly together for several minutes, drinking in the stillness and the sun. It felt like we had entered a "timeless space" and that all we needed to know about our origin and purpose was being answered in that moment. It was a profoundly spiritual experience, and the feeling stayed with me for days.

Several years ago, I spent a summer interviewing men and women on how and when they connect to God or the sacred (I discuss this survey further in chapter 5). Number one on the list for 90 percent of them was spending time in nature. Nature is an incredible source of spiritual, as well as physical, mental, and emotional, renewal and connection. If this resonates with you, consider pursuing one or more of the following opportunities for spiritual renewal in nature:

- TAKE A CONTEMPLATIVE HIKE. Enjoy silent contemplation (defined as a state of mystical awareness of God's being) and reflection on a Sunday morning hike, perhaps in your own "church of the greenbelt"! Or, practice mindfulness anytime — as you walk in a natural area, connect to your breath, and attune to what you hear, smell, taste, touch, and observe.
- BUILD A NATURE ALTAR. Collect some beautiful natural elements from your area (such as pinecones, rosemary, or stones from a creek bed) and create a miniature nature altar in your home — kids love to do this.
- TAKE A LABYRINTH WALK. Find out where the closest labyrinths are in your area and enjoy this ancient "walking meditation" practice, which is designed to help you connect with your inner wisdom.
- JOIN A NATURE RETREAT. Take a retreat with an established group; many churches or spiritual communities offer weekend and weeklong pilgrimages and retreats to beautiful natural areas.
- RECLAIM YOUR ROOTS. Spend time gardening in your yard, or volunteer to help out in someone else's garden or on a local farm; digging in the dirt can be rewarding and healing.
- RETURN HOME. Lie on your back on the ground, fully relax, close your eyes, and allow yourself to be "held" by the earth; surrender and feel your primal connection to your home.
- TAKE A MORNING "NATURE VITAMIN." Enjoy a morning meditation or prayer in your backyard with the birds or on your front porch; have your kids or whole family join you before you begin your day.
- NOURISH AND GIVE THANKS. Invite your family to eat outside (at a table or

on a blanket on the ground) when you're needing more peace and calm; take turns sharing one thing you're grateful for in nature.

Nature has the power to remind us of who we really are, to help us return to our river of well-being, to our Source. Nature helps us "reset" and see what truly matters most.

APPRECIATION and INNER WISDOM: UNEXPECTED GIFTS from NATURE

My whole life I've struggled to find the balance between doing and being. We can easily lose track of the importance of the present moment and even our own inner wisdom when we're caught up in multitasking our busy lives, worrying about tomorrow, and deriving our sense of accomplishment and self-worth from how many balls we're juggling.

One weekend my friend Celeste and I attended a yoga retreat at a Zen Buddhist retreat center on a beautiful old farm, "roughing it" on bunk beds in a room with strangers. For two days, I relaxed and enjoyed long, nourishing yoga sessions, time alone in nature, quiet meditations, and out-of-this-world vegetarian food. On the last night of the retreat, we snuck away to bask under the large, steamy full moon, wrapped in a blanket of sounds: the wind in the trees, coyote howls, even mooing from cows on a distant farm.

Immersing myself in a contemplative natural setting and slowing way down without any responsibilities tugging at my sleeve left me with a deep appreciation for the subtle but powerful beauty of the now. My life isn't last year or next year; it's being breathed and created in this moment. The experience continued even after I returned home: everything seemed brighter, sharper, and more vibrant. The cicadas in the park next to my house sounded like they were preparing to launch into Vivaldi's "Four Seasons." I savored the experience of putting my young son to bed — smelling his clean, just-washed wet hair, holding him tight and feeling his heartbeat, telling him a story about an adventurous wild boy in the woods ("Make it scary, Mama!"), and kissing his sweet soft cheeks.

"It's not a luxury to get away and immerse yourself in a natural setting. It's like oxygen. It's essential to your well-being. It's one of the greatest gifts we have available to us."
— Renée Trudeau

In general, I felt more alive, more attuned to the nuances of my surroundings, and more present and connected to the web of life. There's a deeper invitation within each of us — often revealed when we spend time immersed in nature — to embrace, revel in, and hang out as much as possible in life's mysteries. Nature is an amazing elixir. It has the power to heal, restore, reconnect, and bring us back to each other — and ourselves.

One weekend in the Texas Hill Country, my son, husband, and I climbed the beautiful, majestic Enchanted Rock, a magical, pink granite dome that rises about 425 feet above the gravel trails. After making it to the top, we each chose our own path to descend down the isolated west side of the rock. As we moved slowly, navigating steep slopes and piles of boulders, I reflected on what an individual journey this was for each of us. We each carefully chose where to place our feet and how to negotiate the difficult terrain based on our own comfort, skill level, and physical fitness — but also in large part based on our intuition. We were each allowing our inner wisdom to guide us. As I descended, a work challenge flashed before me, and as it did, the answer and necessary course of action became instantly clear.

Our intuition is our built-in GPS system. Sometimes the guidance we receive from it may not make apparent sense, but I have learned that if I ignore these prompts, I only make things harder. I've come to think of my intuition as a dear, old friend. She is always accessible and never too busy for me. She just sits quietly and waits while I go round and round with my same old story until I'm ready to get quiet and hear her speak the truth.

Nature often opens me to the present moment, so that I can access wisdom and intuitive guidance, tapping into insights I never could have heard before. I never cease to be amazed by the ideas and clarity that often bubble up after a weekend at the ocean or a day in the cool, dark woods.

Just remember to get outside, surrender to this powerful force, and let it work its magic!

Pat on the Back

WHAT'S WORKING?

What is one way you currently encourage your family — or have done so in the past — to spend time in nature?

Putting It into Practice

A GRATITUDE WALK

One of the fastest ways to shift your mood is a gratitude practice. Also, one of the ways that men most enjoy sharing and talking is while walking — there's even science that backs this up! As a family, we love to combine both by taking evening nature walks after dinner, during which we each share three things we're grateful for that week. We've taken our evening strolls in hundred-degree weather and thirty-degree weather. And every time, when we're done, we feel uplifted and full of gratitude for all the blessings in our lives — and our natural environment.

After your own gratitude walk, consider these questions: What did you observe, and how did this affect you? How did it change how you and your family relate to one another? Did you notice any gifts from this experience? Share them in your journal or a notebook.

Imagine a New Way of Being

A JOURNALING EXERCISE

Close your eyes for a minute and place one hand over the center of your chest. Take a deep breath. Observe with curiosity and compassion whatever thoughts and feelings this chapter has stirred up for you. When you're ready, explore the following:

- What would it look like for your family to spend more time in nature — when and how would this work best for you?
- How would it feel — what might the benefits be — if you spent more time in the great outdoors?
- How might your family relationships shift if you consciously chose to spend more time together in nature? Are you willing to change your schedule or drop old habits — like Saturday morning donut runs — to make this a priority?

PAUSE for PEACE
Life Breathes Me

One day at yoga, my teacher said, "Life breathes me." *Wow*, I thought, *we're being breathed — even though we think we're doing all the work?!* I love this concept. It helps me surrender and feel more connected to my true self. Put your hand over the center of your chest, connect with your breath and heartbeat, and slowly breathe in and out through your nose (with your mouth closed). Inhale deeply for three, hold for three, then exhale out for three. Repeat at least three times, or as many times as you like. It is said that the breath is the bridge between our humanity and our divinity. Nothing connects us to our true essence and helps us remember who we really are more than breathing.

Chapter 5

RETURNING to the RIVER: FINDING SPIRITUAL RENEWAL

It's 1976, *and my mom and dad are sitting quietly with their eyes closed, hands resting upward — thumb and index finger touching — while my younger siblings crawl on their backs and shoulders. My older two brothers and I sit quietly, holding our own meditation poses, bored, rolling our eyes and counting the minutes until this ritual will end.*

Against the back wall of the Peterson family meditation room, which is through two French doors to the left of our house's entryway, sits a life-size fourteenth-century, hand-carved nativity scene from Germany, small bronze and wooden statues of Indian deities, and Greek iconic artwork of various saints. Rosary and mala prayer beads are strewn around the floor, and faded gold-and-red meditation cushions are scattered across the room (usually nestled on a spray of Cheerios), while throughout the house, among and around the toy-covered, green-plaid couch and scattered musical instruments, are endless shelves of books on topics ranging from anatomy and physiology to Buddhism.

At least once a week or whenever things get stressful, my parents pull all five of their children — ranging in age from ten to one — into this space for a family meditation.

I complain incessantly about these sessions (what ten-year-old wants to meditate?!), but a deeper part of me resonates with the quiet, the invitation to do nothing but sit, and the smell of frankincense that my dad often burns on a small handmade wood altar that sits under the sunny east window.

My parents exposed my siblings and me to numerous religious paths growing up. My mom was raised Presbyterian, my dad Methodist. They were always drawn to mysticism, and they converted to Catholicism after their second child. Beginning in the early 1970s, Eastern spiritual teachings began playing a pivotal role in their lives, particularly Hinduism and Buddhism. I have a sister named after St. Teresa and a brother named after Shiva (the Hindu "destroyer and transformer"), and my siblings' godparents include nuns, priests, swamis, and ministers — many of whom we broke bread with over long meals and philosophical discussions often late into the evening.

True seekers, my parents were constantly questioning how and where they could feel closer to God. As dysfunctional as my family was, my parents understood that spiritual nourishment was as essential to their individual and family's well-being and health as good nutrition and exercise. In fact, sometimes their focus on nourishing our souls overshadowed everything else.

Lately, when I speak on the topic of self-care to large groups and introduce the four areas of renewal — physical, mental, emotional, and spiritual — many people share that they feel their greatest area of need is in the spiritual arena. Surprised? In fact, over the past fifteen years, I've heard many clients express a recurring dissatisfaction or boredom with their lives. Some say their lives are, technically speaking or superficially, "fine." They're healthy, have hobbies, like their work, and spend time with their families, and yet they feel that something is missing. In countless conversations, people express that what they most need and want is to live a purposeful life, one ripe with meaning and a deep sense of connection to themselves, to others, and to God (or a higher power). They want to feel their lives matter, to experience heartfelt community and know that they "belong." And they desire to revel in the mystery of life, to know that life is more than a "thing to be managed." Ultimately, I believe our need for spiritual nourishment or renewal is tied to our desire to feel connected to something bigger than ourselves — we want to sense our *oneness* with the Divine or the universe. This sense of malaise or dissatisfaction is what leads us to start exploring life *from the inside out*. When there is unrest, we want an anchor, just like our children want their security blankets. The desire for a safe harbor is prompting us to search out ways to enhance our sense of inner peace and connection to the Divine. I believe it's our birthright and responsibility to nurture our inner world, our connection to Spirit, and to create space for spiritual renewal through the paths of reflection, contemplation, stillness, ritual, service to others, and spiritual community.

> "God is everywhere —
> in the creek behind our home,
> in our family members' eyes,
> in the stars overhead, in the stories
> we share at dinner — just waiting
> to be experienced."
> — Renée Trudeau

As I mention in chapter 4, a couple of years back I dedicated a summer to researching the topic of everyday spirituality. I was very curious to learn where and how people find connection to the Divine in their day-to-day lives, if at all. I interviewed a diverse group of sixty men and women (ages twenty-eight to sixty-six) and challenged them to stretch beyond their beliefs or assumptions — such as that to experience God they must join a Zen monastery, sit in a pew, go on a retreat in Bali, or meditate or pray for three hours a day. I wanted to know how and when people connect to the Divine — while they're unloading the dishwasher, grocery shopping, disciplining their child, driving carpools, meeting with coworkers, or helping their kids with homework.

I was overwhelmed with the enthusiastic and thoughtful responses from the people who agreed to participate in my survey. They shared their "doorways" for connecting to God or the sacred in the everyday. Here are the main ones:

- Spending time in nature was number one for the majority of people.
- Some people cited body movement, whether that was dance, breath work, qi gong, yoga, or jogging.

- Prayer and meditation included any practice in which people consciously took time to connect with the Divine.
- Many mentioned simply living in the present by embracing this moment and releasing the past and future.
- Service to others, or being in an intentional community working with a group toward a larger goal, put many people in touch with their interconnectedness. One example was assembling a jungle gym for their school.
- Many also mentioned practicing simple acts of gratitude: regular, spoken or unspoken moments of deep appreciation.
- For some, artistic expression was high on their list: singing, playing an instrument, painting, writing, and sculpting.
- Playing with their babies or small children helped some experience pure joy in the "now."

Surprisingly, of the respondents who said nature was their number one path for experiencing God, only a small number said they regularly spent time in nature. Most acknowledged that being in a spiritual community was beneficial, but you don't have to go to church or gather with others to feel God, although personally I find it really nice to have this support for our family, particularly as our son moves into his teens.

Sometimes we may think we need to create "special conditions" or visit sacred places to connect to our spiritual nature, but God is everywhere — in the creek behind our home, in our family members' eyes, in the stars overhead, in the stories we share at dinner — just waiting to be experienced.

What are your portals for spiritual renewal — those things your soul needs to be nourished? Do you consciously take time to feed your spirit through these pathways?

SELF-CARE as SPIRITUAL PRACTICE

Last year I facilitated an intimate women's circle focused on self-care as a spiritual practice in which we explored the connection between self-compassion, self-care, and our ability to feel God in the everyday. During the three-month program, the women — all moms at different life stages — noticed a strong correlation. When we practiced self-care and nurtured ourselves with the deepest compassion, our connection to the Divine became more real and present, too. *Loving ourselves made us feel closer to God.*

Taking this into the real world, group members observed and recorded how and when they felt God (or their spiritual equivalent for God) in their everyday life. What happened surprised us all. When we slowed down, attuned, and responded to our needs and practiced self-kindness and self-nurturance, we experienced a profound sense of sacredness and connection to Spirit in our daily interactions.

- Single mom Mary's parenting shifted and became "Zen-like" when she slowed down, stopped multitasking, became more present, and took time to "see" and play with her young kids.
- When Kathy paused to look up and connect with the checker in the grocery store — without mechanically rushing through the line — it completely opened her heart and changed the tone of her entire day.
- Elizabeth practiced compassion for herself and others by reaching out to another parent on the school playground who was clearly having a hard day, and she felt a tidal wave of positive energy flow through her.
- Erin noticed that when she focused on gratitude during her workday and took time to acknowledge her coworkers' innate goodness, she felt much more connected to humanity.
- When Julie danced — not because she had to, but for pure pleasure — she could feel Spirit alive in her body and bones.
- Alisa walked outside one night to gaze at the stars, and by doing so, she felt perceptibly closer to God and more connected to her essence.
- Jane and her kids hiked in a park near their home one morning and

sat quietly next to a waterfall for a few minutes of silence; they could feel a connection to one another *and* to the larger web of life.

The women all described feeling a heightened sense of interconnectedness — to themselves and to others — during these moments. This exercise helped us to tap into that rare but magical quality of "oneness" — that sense that we're much more alike than we are different — which most of us have tasted at one time or another.

Following the path of self-care to the road of self-acceptance has been life changing. Every day I unwrap the gifts that come from this spiritual practice, including a much healthier outlook about body image.

When I celebrated my forty-fifth birthday, I felt a strong pull to nest, rest, and reflect, and after enjoying a massage and a hot aromatherapy bath, I was inspired to write a letter of appreciation to my dear old friend.

Dear 45-year-old body:

I love you. I really do. I'm sorry it has taken me so long to arrive at this place.

I love you, radiant face that gets more interesting and playful the older you get (and fascinating neck — it seems as if you're developing a personality of your own!).

I love you, sweet soft belly, just the way you are. And I'm amazed by your ability to grow a child that is now up to my chin!

I love you, full, sweet, strong upper arms that give great hugs, will never be willowy, and were inherited from Grandma Harrison (so I'm told).

I love you, hands (Grandma Nonnie's hands), and the way you have supported me in writing, painting, expressing myself musically, cooking, and serving others.

I love you, amazing feet — hail to the feet! You've carried me for thousands of miles from Big Sur to Egypt, from Oaxaca to Ephesus, and around Lady Bird Lake twice a week for the past twenty years.

I love you, sweet, healthy breasts that have helped me embrace my femininity and have brought me from maiden to motherhood to middle age (oh the stories you hold!).

I love you, sometimes cranky, but always lovable knees — especially the small crinkles that are just starting to crash the party and how they suddenly make their entrance when I do a downward dog in yoga class.

Sweet body, I so appreciate how you house my soul and allow me to experience pleasure and express love to those around me. I promise to continue to listen and respond to your needs and desires in the coming years and will do my best to love you through all the changes and evolutions that are yet to come.

Much love and deep gratitude—

Your best friend, Renée

PARENTING as a SPIRITUAL PATH

My dad began a daily meditation practice when I was five; he loved to travel and attend long, usually ten-day silent meditation retreats. I remember my mom getting angry when he left to attend one of these right after the birth of their fourth child, my brother Sean. My dad studied the world's great religions and spiritual traditions, and he sat at the feet of swamis, priests, therapists, authors, and theologians — but the more he went outward, the more he missed what was right in front of him the whole time: the achingly mundane but sweet, vast, and profound landscape called family.

Conscious parenting is some of the most intense spiritual work I've ever done. Many parents find that having a child is a profound wake-up call to explore their own spiritual nature and to ask questions they may have never considered. This was clearly the case with my parents.

Maya, mom to five-year-old twins, shares, "The other day my son Ethan very assuredly told me, 'Mom, I think we need to find a church to go to today. I have something I need to say to God, and Bode [his classmate] said, if I want to talk to God, I have to go to church.'" My friend Delia's eight-year-old daughter, Eliana, asked her mom every morning for weeks after her maternal grandmother died, "But Mama, where is Nana? You said she's still with us, but I can't see her!" Our kids provide us with great opportunities for spiritual exploration, ours as well as theirs, whether we're ready for it or not! Whatever we need to work on — patience, compassion, self-love, gratitude, acceptance — our kids will ensure we have the opportunity to explore this part of our nature.

> "We've created 'home church,' where we listen to or watch an inspirational or thought-provoking message, lecture, or sermon together and then discuss it. It's a great way to let everyone's ideas be heard."
> — Richard, 42, father of three

A few years back, my husband and I took the How to Talk So Kids Will Listen and Listen So Kids Will Talk parenting course, based on the book by Adele Faber and Elaine Mazlish. One evening after coming home from class, I was filled with deep feelings of gratitude for the opportunity to be a mother to this sweet, wonderful soul and to be his pupil (even when he challenges me to my limit!). Later that night after putting Jonah to bed, I wrote him a thank-you letter acknowledging how much he's taught me about forgiveness, trusting, starting over, softening, releasing, stretching, and expanding. For inspiring me to give birth to the best that is within me. No matter where we are on our spiritual journey, having a child accelerates our personal growth and provides us with numerous avenues for self-discovery and life learning.

Over the years I've heard from many men and women on the spiritual gifts they've received from parenthood. These include

- AN INCREASED CAPACITY TO LOVE. For many, love expands, deepens, and widens after becoming a parent — it's as if we have a Grinch moment and our hearts swell!
- A DEEPER SENSE OF COMPASSION FOR OTHERS. I remember one day talking to a gruff, tattoo-covered convenience store clerk who was having a hard time and thinking, as Jonah cooed in his sling, *This man is someone's baby boy.*
- INCREASED UNDERSTANDING FOR THE CHALLENGES OTHER PARENTS FACE. Often we tap into more empathy for the challenges

and issues single parents, low-income parents, and parents of children with special needs face.

- AN APPRECIATION FOR THE NOW. There is nothing that brings you into the present moment like a toddler who wants to stop every two feet to look at caterpillars or blades of grass.
- A RENEWED SENSE OF JOY IN LIFE. Now available on the menu every day — if you choose. Just watch your baby's eyes light up when she sees you walk into the room or gets her first balloon.
- A SHIFT IN PRIORITIES. What's really important in life often become crystal clear: we see what's essential, what would be "nice to do," and what needs to fall off our list or wait until later.
- A NEW SENSE OF MORAL RESPONSIBILITY. Our desire to model our best selves, and even our sense of integrity, often increases as we become teachers to our children. I remember visiting a museum when Jonah was a toddler. As we paid for our admission, the woman behind the counter said, "Oh, two-year-olds are free." I started to move ahead without thinking, when I realized she was talking about my son. Feeling the "angel of ethics" on my shoulder, I plunked two dollars down on the counter. "Actually, he just turned three," I said, smiling.
- FINDING YOUR VOICE. Many women claim they first found their voice after becoming mothers, perhaps because we're required to state our children's need to others when they're not yet able to speak. Do you find it easier to speak your truth after having kids?

SPIRITUAL NOURISHMENT: FOOD for the SOUL

Regardless of your beliefs, spiritual nourishment and renewal are essential to your overall emotional well-being. "Soul food" helps us nurture our essence, feel centered, build inner strength, live in integrity, trust life, experience a connection to a higher power, feel a sense of purpose, and experience meaning in our lives. Spiritual nourishment is like compost; it's the super-charged, nutrient-dense soil for our "inner world." When we don't get this, we wither on the vine.

The road to awakening — and the spiritual journey — will look different for each of us. One night while cleaning out my clothes closet, I listened to a radio interview hosting a panel of experts talking about spirituality. A recurring theme the panel touched on — which I hear many parents discuss — is how a religious upbringing sometimes scares people away from talking or thinking about God or being part of a spiritual community. Is this true for you? How has your upbringing affected how you view religion and spirituality now? As a parent, do you feel a new (or renewed) desire to explore your spiritual nature? Do you want to integrate spiritual practice more fully into your everyday family life?

There are many different ways to explore and nurture our spiritual lives on a day-to-day basis. Some of the paths or teachings that most deeply feed my soul include what I call the "six portals" to spiritual nourishment:

PORTAL 1: Creating ritual
PORTAL 2: Cultivating stillness
PORTAL 3: Developing acceptance for what is
PORTAL 4: Practicing service to others
PORTAL 5: Living in the present
PORTAL 6: Choosing happiness

I invite you to explore these six portals in greater depth. Keep an open mind and see which ones call to you.

Portal 1: Creating Ritual

We all crave sacredness and ritual in our everyday lives — not just around birthdays, Bar Mitzvahs, and weddings. Rituals can be both carefully planned events and casual but regular remembrances. Cultivating the latter can be as simple as voicing gratitude before a meal, creating regular space in your day for contemplation, setting an intention before a yoga or movement class, scheduling morning and/or evening meditations, lighting a special candle in your home or work space before you start the day, or creating family "support circles" in which you take turns sharing your needs. One of our family's favorite rituals is hosting a "back-to-school" blessing for the kids in our neighborhood. We gather in a circle on the back porch after a special meal and have the kids voice and write down a one-word theme or intention for the coming school year, and then all the parents shower them with positive qualities — focus, compassion, the ability to try new things — for a healthy, enjoyable year. I also like to celebrate the Mexican holiday tradition of All Souls' Day (November 2); I set up a Day of the Dead altar to honor deceased relatives. My son loves to be involved in this ritual.

I also recommend creating larger rituals that celebrate important life transitions. For instance, when my sister was thirty and pregnant with her first child, I hosted a blessingway — a ceremony derived from a Navajo tradition. (In Native American culture, women are honored as they pass through many phases in life, not just pregnancy.) I have always related to my sister as a blend of sister, mother, and mentor; I was fourteen when she was born, and she was only a teenager when our parents died. But our relationship is slowly changing. About twelve women, both friends and relatives, attended the ceremony. None had ever attended a blessingway before, and it was a new and unusual experience for them to come together with other women in such an intimate way.

I spent hours Sunday morning getting ready for the gathering. Being about as noncrafty as they come, I was very proud when I successfully hobbled together a simple handmade flower wreath to adorn my sister's head. For me, the process of contemplatively preparing for my sister's arrival that Sunday felt like a ritual unto itself.

Then, when everyone had arrived, we gathered in a circle on cushions on the floor in our front room. I told stories about growing up with four brothers and how excited I was when the "surprise twins" made their entry — and one of them was a girl! I talked about the significance of women's circles, my sister's journey from maiden to mother, and the importance of asking for and receiving help from a tribe. Then we all took turns "gifting" my sister with qualities to support her as a new mother and honoring her beautiful, kind, generous, and wise heart. As we took turns sharing, we created a birthing necklace for my sister by stringing together carefully chosen, symbolic charms and beads. Finally, we blessed "birthing" candles that each woman left with and that they would light as soon as they received word that my sister's labor had begun. Many of the women were visibly moved by this ceremony; it was clear that many were starved for this level and type of connection.

When we mark important transitions or milestones in our lives — whether it's your daughter's first period or your son starting kindergarten — we connect to the sacredness of life in the everyday. We remember that life is mysterious and unknown — and way more than a to-do list. Rituals help remind us that we're all swimming in the same big, vast, miraculous, and awe-inspiring ocean.

Portal 2: Cultivating Stillness

Stillness, whether experienced through prayer, meditation, or reflection, is our time to be alone and connect to our inner wisdom or our higher power — what I call our internal GPS system. I think it's essential for all of us to carve out time for reflection each day — ideally, first thing in the morning, when our minds are most quiet. If our outer world is a reflection of our inner world, don't you want to take time to weed and care for your inner garden?

Perhaps you already know how life changing meditation can be. Amy, a retreat participant, once compared the difference between meditating and not meditating to the difference between wearing shoes and walking barefoot. The days she meditates in the morning — whether for five minutes in the car after dropping her kids at school or for twenty minutes before she starts her workday — she feels grounded, protected, and more at ease. The little things don't turn into big things quite so easily. When she doesn't meditate, she feels barefoot and exposed. When she steps on pebbles, she gets irritated more easily. She's not as relaxed or trusting, and when she encounters the inevitable, unexpected obstacles in her path, she's more easily thrown off course. I can relate. When I meditate, I find I flow with the day instead of pushing against it.

If we know that taking time to meditate, pray, and quiet our minds has such a huge impact on our well-being, why don't we do it regularly, all the time? Why do we always create distractions and avoid being still?

For years, I fought this idea of a morning ritual, of creating dedicated time every day to get quiet before entering the world. I rationalized: "It's too hard when you're a parent, and I'm too busy. I'll do it later in the day. I would, but my husband won't join me. I don't have the right space. I need a new meditation cushion." And so on. I worked hard to justify my reluctance, always wondering, "Does it really make a difference?" Today, it seems crazy that I needlessly postponed what I now consider the single most important part of my day.

If you don't currently meditate but are curious about how meditating might impact your well-being, start by approaching this as an experiment. Try it for a short time and see for yourself what kind of difference it makes for you. I once heard Marianne Williamson, the internationally known modern mystic and bestselling author of *A Return to Love*, say on a radio interview that devoting as little as five minutes every morning to your inner life can set a positive course for your entire day. As I had battled for years trying to commit to a daily twenty-minute meditation practice, this wisdom really spoke to me. Being grateful every morning for five minutes? I could do that.

Within stillness lies great wisdom and answers. We just have to get quiet enough and be willing to create the space to allow this to come through. For many, meditation is the secret weapon for maintaining our sanity! Here are five tips for beginning and building a meditation practice:

- SCHEDULE MEDITATION FOR THE SAME TIME EACH DAY. It works best to meditate early in the morning, since this is often when the house is the most quiet — such as before anyone else is up or immediately after everyone else has left for school and work. The morning is also when our minds are most quiet and clear. If you're not an early-morning person, do it later in the day: take a midmorning nature break while at work, or wait until after the kids have gone to bed. Or, integrate your meditation into a morning movement practice — such as yoga, tai chi, or qi gong.

- IDENTIFY WHERE YOU'LL PAUSE FOR YOUR PRACTICE. Identify or create a space in your home that elicits peace, healing, and self-nurturance. Know that you can go there at any time, and use this as a regular meditation place. Maybe it's a special reading chair, a creativity altar, or a spot in the backyard under your favorite tree. Or, if setting aside a certain spot isn't feasible, simply close your office or bedroom door to create a temporary "space." Identify a quiet parking lot or a nearby green space where you can park alone during your morning commute. Get creative!

- USE A SOURCE OF COMFORT AND INSPIRATION. To focus their intention and set the tone for the day, many like to read and meditate on an inspirational text or phrase. This could be from a spiritual teaching, the Bible, a favorite book or poem, or even an inspirational card deck (many spiritual teachers and authors offer these). Check out www.dailyword.com and www.dailyom.com for more.

- REMEMBER TO BREATHE. Sometimes when we meditate, our agitation and anxieties fill our heads with thoughts and to-do lists. When this happens, don't forget to breathe! Breathing detoxifies, energizes, changes our mood and biochemistry, wakes up the brain, and helps us feel more present and calm. One technique I use when meditating is to breathe in very slowly for a count of three, hold for three, and exhale for three — all through the nose with the mouth closed. Keeping your eyes closed while doing this also helps focus your awareness inward.

- RITUALIZE YOUR MORNING MEDITATION TIME. Establish a simple ritual or routine for your morning meditation, which provides a rhythm and structure. For example, you might first light a candle, close your eyes, and rest in stillness. If you like, you could then read a short inspirational text, and close by reflecting on what you're grateful for or setting an intention for the day. You might ask for guidance on an issue or help releasing feelings that have been bothering you. Choose a rhythm and flow that works for you.

For your morning practice to have the greatest effect, release "shoulds" or "have tos." There is no right or wrong way to do this. Create a ritual you enjoy, keep it simple, maintain a sense of humor, and — above all — make it personally meaningful.

Joan, a meditation teacher I know, says, "How do you know when you've had a successful meditation? It's over. Don't worry about the results. Just creating the space for stillness and accepting whatever unfolds is enough! Every time you come to your cushion will be different." Allow yourself to experience what it's like to be fully present and comfortable sitting in silence. And be easy on yourself. If this is new, even just starting with five minutes of quiet before you begin your day is huge!

Lastly, give this time. You may not experience immediate or consistent results, but you still receive tremendous benefit from regular practice. Even on the days when my thoughts are ricocheting around like exploding popcorn, I still feel better after I meditate than I did before I arrived on my meditation cushion. Susan, a single mom, says, "There are days when my morning time is in the car with my son on the way to school. We do a quick check in and together set intentions for what kind of day we want to experience. Even this makes a big difference."

If you're ready to experience lasting change in your life and tap into inner peace on a daily basis, develop and stick with a daily spiritual practice. A spiritual mentor once said to me, "Want to experience a little bit of peace? Meditate once a week. Want to experience a lot of peace? Meditate every day."

Portal 3: Developing Acceptance for What Is

One of the biggest gifts I've received from meditation is the ability to live more comfortably with "what is." Life is like the weather in Texas — constantly changing. Temperatures shift wildly and unexpected thunderstorms suddenly blow through. Meditation has helped anchor me, so that despite this impermanence and turmoil, I've learned how to be still and find my center in the face of it all.

When I have time, I really enjoy nurturing my family and myself by cooking great meals, using a lot of local, fresh produce from area farms. One night I planned a special dinner of citrus-and-shallot swordfish, rice with toasted sesame seeds, sautéed garlic eggplant, and fresh pineapple. Then we sat down to eat and discovered the swordfish was bad and the eggplant was bitter. So our dinner consisted of rice and pineapple! My disappointment turned to laughter, and my husband, son, and I ended up finishing our simple meal and heading outside for a walk.

We create pain, despair, and sadness when we disagree with reality. Once we learn to question our own thoughts and stories — and create more space around how we react — we begin to understand that the world is our perception of it. We see and hear through the filter of our individual "lens." When was the last time you cleaned yours?

We have a finite amount of energy available to us each day. When we get stuck fighting "what is," we waste our precious energy on what we can't change instead of focusing on what we can. Perhaps we struggle with our current state of unemployment, chronic pain, an astronomical credit card bill, a car accident, or a too-busy life. We can't change what's already happened, but we can change our perspective and how we choose to experience what happens tomorrow — whether that's a career change, nurturing our relationships and being present with our kids, getting our financial house in order, growing our business, and so on. Years ago, the smallest thing — an error on a phone bill, a work decision I "perceived" as not going my way, an argument with a family member — would really throw me. Sometimes for days! I wasted so much energy fighting "what was" and ruminating about how things might be different. These types of incidences would send me into a downward spiral of negative thought, centering on the mantra "Everything's going wrong!"

Yet even when things do seem to go wrong, what else can you do but handle the problem in front of you and move on? I remember one weekend in which my new car suffered a hit-and-run while parked in front of a Japa-nese restaurant (causing three thousand dollars in damage), and my husband's car — which had just been in the shop — started leaking gas and needed a fourteen-hundred-dollar fuel tank replacement. Just like that, our budget was blown, and our schedule was in shambles: my husband had to take a long bus ride to his office all week, while I juggled morning meetings and school drop-offs and pick-ups.

Naturally, we were frustrated and annoyed. But after years of practice not resisting what is, we've finally learned to handle what comes up and move on. We'd rather make peace with our problems, and feel peace in ourselves, than fight what is and continue feeling bad.

We still have a long way to go, and I often challenge myself — and my thinking — to notice how long I stay stuck, and how long it takes me to question my perception about a situation that initially looks "bad." Spiritual teacher Byron Katie said at a workshop I attended, "Arguing with reality is like trying to teach a cat to bark — hopeless."

Peace is only a thought away. Feeling good is just a matter of stretching and anchoring into a better-feeling place — if you're willing to challenge, and transcend, your own thoughts.

Portal 4: Practicing Service to Others

For the front of my mom's brown-flecked funeral service program, I chose the quote by Mother Teresa, "The fruit of love is service, which is compassion in action."

This quote really captures the best of my mom. She wasn't perfect and struggled with self-acceptance, but she was incredibly compassionate toward others, whether friends or strangers. My parents felt strongly about serving and giving to others, and I have many memories of their efforts. They took kids from the local orphanage out with us on Sunday family outings; they generously supported a family in our church community whose house had burned down; they would buy a hundred boxes of Girl Scout cookies to give to neighbors; and they once purchased a refrigerator for our Laotian babysitter — a single mother raising five children.

On the one hand, many of us care deeply about the many problems and atrocities afflicting our society and the world, but it's easy to get overwhelmed. We turn away or shut down and do nothing, thinking, "What can I as an individual really do that will make a difference?"

Then again, many of us do choose to jump in and get involved in a whole variety of ways, big and small. Sometimes, though, we become so focused on helping others and the disenfranchised that we miss the many opportunities to serve those right next to us who desperately need our help. These overlooked people could be our spouse, our children, our parents and relatives, and our friends and acquaintances. They could be the friend who has two kids with special needs and hasn't had an overnight trip away with her husband in seven years, the coworker's sister who just got divorced and is struggling to find work, the mom in your book club who just needs some-one to really listen and be present for her, the recent college graduate who is struggling with depression and needs referrals for support, or the young Korean boy in your son's kindergarten class who just moved here and is hav-ing a hard time making friends. Serving those closest to us — in our families and local communities — is a powerful way to serve the world.

We are all interconnected. The more we reach out and are present to one another's pain and suffering, the stronger we become and the easier it is to embrace the esoteric idea that we're all one. I believe ulti-mately a huge shift in consciousness can occur — not when everyone meditates together an hour each day, although that would certainly help — but when everyone takes it upon them-selves to reach out and help one another navigate this sometimes scary, often isolat-ing and perplexing, but ultimately beauti-ful world.

"We encourage our children to feel connected with others by giving time and support to those in need — sometimes that's neighbors whose house burned down and sometimes that's through our local children's shelter."
— Valerie, 52,
mother of three

In addition, our kids are always watch-ing all we do and deciding through these ob-servations who they want to be in the world. I had never really made the connection between how strongly my mom and dad's actions and attitudes affected my perspective on service and volunteerism until I became a parent.

My youngest brother, Tim — who was only a teenager when both our parents passed — majored in religion and community building at Emory University. Many evenings of his freshman year were spent in Atlanta's underground subway, handing out sandwiches to the homeless.

One winter, after months of begging from my then-six-year-old son, we finally pulled it together to volunteer on a Mobile Loaves and Fishes truck — an amazing national nonprofit that feeds and clothes the homeless and poor. On a cold, dark January night, we traveled to halfway homes and gov-ernment housing, offering meals, support, and a little conversation to our neighbors on the other side of town.

Later, my son couldn't stop talking about the experience. He had served homeless men directly from the back of the truck, offering them their choice of sandwiches, fruit, chips, and warm socks. He told me, "Mom, this was the best day of my life!" He later shared with my husband, as he was tucking him in that night, that he used to think the homeless were different from him, but he now realized they're his brothers and sisters.

For many of us, serving and helping one another not only can bring more meaning to our lives and a heightened connection to one another but also can provide a powerful experience of our own divine nature.

Portal 5: Living in the Present

My parents were big fans of author and spiritual teacher Ram Dass, and when their *older* children would get bored and beg to be taken to the movies or the mall, they often responded by telling us to "Be here now!" That directive hardly registered in my teenage ears, nor did any of us succeed at it very often or for very long, but Lord knows my parents tried.

The phrase "be here now" flooded back to me one weekend as I sat on the couch with a nasty full-body cold and wanting to be...anywhere but where I was. Sick. At home. Immobile.

So many stress-management gurus and spiritual teachers believe the answer to everything is to just "be here now" or to "be with what is." Many of them say all suffering and emotional distress would end if we simply stopped resisting being in the moment. If we embraced the "now." I agree with this principle, but it's challenging, especially when your head is about to split in two, your body feels like wet spaghetti, and your nose is running like a faucet. But I know that discomfort often brings amazing gifts, so I explored what would happen if I stopped resisting my uninvited house guest, Franny Flu.

As I watched the things I was missing fly out the window — my friend's creativity party, my son's piano recital, working on the garden, cleaning my office — and surrendered, connected to my breath, and felt myself arrive in the present moment, I could feel my resistance dissipate. A sense of peace and quiet slowly settled over me. I temporarily suspended my desire for things to be different, and as I released my expectations about relationships, work, and obligations, out went their siblings: worry, anxiety, and stress.

On the couch with a head cold was exactly where I was supposed to be.

Be here now. As my dad would say, "You never know when you'll bump up against enlightenment." It might even reside at the bottom of a Kleenex box.

Portal 6: Choosing Happiness

I was having dinner with friends late last year. Most of us were experiencing various stages of disequilibrium in our lives — my husband had just gotten laid off from his tech job, my friend was navigating a divorce, and my neighbor's house was being foreclosed.

My friend Susan asked me, "So, how are you?" I paused for a minute, then replied, "Actually, I'm great. I'm feeling really good." She looked at me with confusion. She didn't understand how I could be doing well when I was navigating so many personal challenges.

"I think happiness is a choice, and in this moment, this day, this is how I'm choosing to feel," I replied.

I didn't always make this choice. Three of my immediate family members died unexpectedly between my twenty-sixth and thirty-fourth birthdays. Throughout most of my twenties and into my early thirties, I let those losses dictate how much, how often, and when I could experience joy. For years, anytime I started to feel light, free, or happy, the old feeling of "waiting for the other shoe to drop" would creep in.

We all want to be happy, but where does happiness come from? To be happy, do we need things to be perfect, so that the feeling flutters down upon us like a butterfly on a sun-drenched, perfect-temperature, not-a-cloud-in-the-sky day? Or can we learn to be happy despite our imperfections and old wounds? Haven't we all played the "I'll be happy when..." game? I'll be happy when I've finished my project, have a new job, graduated school, finalized my divorce, gotten paid, figured out my life purpose...and on and on. Can you only be happy if things are going your way and all the stars are aligned in your favor? In recent years, there's been a lot of focus on the psychology of happiness, and one thing is clear: happiness isn't something that

happens to us; it's something we create. At an international coaching conference, I heard author and teacher Tal Ben-Shahar discuss how much power
we have over our ability to be happy. We create our happiness when we help
others, express gratitude, live more in the present, and take time for soul-
nourishing, deeply absorbing work and activities. Conversely — surprise,
surprise — true happiness is not derived from the accumulation of "stuff"
or the typical pleasures and gratifications we often pursue.

I believe that we're born with the innate capacity to experience emotional well-being and joy; it's our birthright to feel good. God wants us to
feel good. Most of us just forget this as we head out into the wooded forest to
search for Pandora's box, certain that the secret to happiness has to be "out
there"...somewhere.

On my son's last day of third grade, we hosted an end-of-year school
party. Moments after everyone had arrived, my husband called to let me
know he'd just been laid off from his tech job. Summer is my favorite time
of year. I love the fresh peaches and basil, I love cold swims in our local rivers, I love reading and more reading, and I love enjoying a slower pace with
my family. I wanted to be supportive of my partner and fully on board to
take over as the primary provider for my family for a while, but if I spent
the entire summer preoccupied with worry and
going into a "spin cycle" over our finances, summer would pass me by. I'd wake up on Labor Day
having missed some of the best days of the year!

So I consciously decided that just because life
had thrown us a curveball didn't mean we had to
stop living. That summer of unemployment included some challenges, but it also included making frozen blueberry-banana smoothies on a stick
(my son's invention), late-evening picnics, refreshing swims in Texas's natural springs, and some of the most tender, connected, joyful moments my
family has ever experienced. It helped that we'd been through a layoff one
time before, and we knew this was merely a bump in the road.

Happiness bubbles up from our spring of well-being (which needs tend-
ing to flow). We're wired for happiness. We just have to remember to choose
this and consciously return here moment to moment. I was once challenged

by my friend Erin, a leadership coach, to "think a better thought!" When we can see how our negative thoughts and our state of being are contributing to our unhappiness — shifts can occur.

Grab a piece of paper and a pen and write out the top five things that bring you back to a state of joy or happiness. While we feel satisfaction after completing a successful project or we enjoy the momentary high that comes from a promotion or from doing something new and exciting, these things fade and aren't always within our reach. In fact, if we are too focused on pursuing them, they could adversely affect our joy and well-being — such as if they impact our relationships and the amount of time we enjoy with our family.

More and more, I'm realizing that the less I feel I "have to do," and the simpler my life is, the happier I am. The quickest and easiest route to happiness is choosing to reconnect with that inner well of happiness and joy that resides within me.

SPIRITUAL MAINTENANCE

It's easy to forget who we really are. To lose sight of what really matters. To fall asleep and not remember how interconnected we all are. That we're fully human and, at the same time, divine.

A regular spiritual practice — whether that's daily meditation, prayer, involvement in a spiritual community, singing, or volunteer work — serves to anchor us. It grounds us and helps us navigate the challenges we face from just being human. It helps us stay awake.

I once attended a retreat where author and teacher Anita Johnston gave each participant a straight pin as a reminder to "not fall asleep" to our own lives — or to our divine, creative potential. What helps you stay awake and present to your life? Perhaps artistic expression, group meditation, or going on periodic spiritual retreats — take time to discover what this is for you.

When we consciously connect with God or our Source, we bloom into awakened souls, vibrant beings and partners, and conscious parents. We begin to trust the rhythm and flow of life.

Spiritual maintenance — taking time each day to intentionally feed our souls — is what brings us to Source, what returns us to the river. When we remember our innately wise and natural state — when we let go and relax into the beauty of who we are — we experience absolute peace and harmony.

Pat on the Back

WHAT'S WORKING?

What is one thing you're currently doing — or have done in the past — to nurture your own or your family's spiritual life?

Putting It into Practice

MAKING FRIENDS WITH MEDITATION

This month I challenge you to integrate a dedicated morning meditation time into your day. Do this for at least seven consecutive days. You might start with just setting an intention for the day or a short five-minute meditation. If you already meditate in the morning, play with increasing the time or add an evening meditation practice before bed. Observe any changes that start to happen. Do you notice your interactions or relationships shifting? How is your state of being — how do you feel throughout the day? Record any insights and share them with a friend or your partner. Many consider meditation to be their most essential self-care practice.

Putting It into Practice

FINDING SPIRITUAL RENEWAL

To dive even deeper into the topic of spiritual renewal, set aside twenty minutes of uninterrupted quiet time to meditate on and answer these questions. Have your partner and child answer them, too, if appropriate.

- What gives my life meaning?
- What is one thing I do for spiritual nourishment? What is one thing my family does?

- To me, God (or the sacred) is...
- I connect to God (or the sacred) through...
- I feel most peaceful when I...

When you finish, set up a family date night to share and discuss your responses (use your judgment on the best time and way to do this based on the age of your kids). Many find that just reflecting on these questions can inspire aha's and deep meaningful conversations about how to incorporate sacredness or spiritual renewal into their everyday lives.

 Imagine a New Way of Being

A JOURNALING EXERCISE

Close your eyes for a minute and place one hand over the center of your chest. Take a deep breath. Observe with curiosity and compassion whatever thoughts and feelings this chapter has stirred up for you. When you're ready, explore the following:

- What might it look like for your family to connect to God or the sacred in everyday life?
- What would it feel like to experience a connection to Source in your everyday life?
- How might your family life shift if you began to nourish yourselves spiritually?

Part III

LOVE THE ONES
YOU'RE WITH

PAUSE for PEACE
A Parent's Mantra

Words are powerful and can have an enormous impact on how we perceive a situation. We often tell our kids, "If you think you can, you can, and if you think you can't, you can't." What's your internal dialogue? Take a moment to pause and put your hands over the center of your chest. Take some deep belly breaths. Now choose a mantra for the day — a phrase or affirmation that helps put you in an empowered and positive frame of mind. Some examples are "I have all the time and support I need," "Everything is working out for the best," and "My life flows with ease." Write your mantra down, post it in your kitchen or office, and carry it into your day, repeating frequently. Use your mantra for a week and see how you feel.

Chapter 6

SPENDING TIME TOGETHER (LIKE YOU MEAN IT!)

People often say, "You can pick your friends, but you can't pick your family." Is that really true? It's a mystery how and why we're together — but it's not a mistake. Your family and everything about you is unique — there will never be another tribe just like yours. Being together in the moment, letting everything else go, and having the opportunity to see, hear, and learn from one another are some of the greatest gifts we'll ever know.

There were many gifts I received from the process of writing this book. One of them was the poem below, which came to me one Friday morning at Whole Foods, while I was sitting with a cup of green tea and preparing to dive back into this chapter. I noticed a family with young kids sitting next to me sharing muffins and having beautiful, tender moments with each other — as if each person were a "just-discovered" treasure. I was overcome with the profound mystery of how and why our souls come together in family and the realization of what a blessing this truly is.

SOULPOD

Here we are. Together again. Sharing lentil soup. Legs tangled, snuggling under the warm blanket. Negotiating piano practice and chores. Telling stories from our day. Moving from asleep to awake and awake to asleep. Navigating being human.

When I stop, I see your curious eyes and your beautiful spirits. You remind me of who I want to be in the world...who I really am.

We have the gift of now. It's a large, beautiful moment. It can expand into the skies and go on forever. We don't need to go to the mountains or the beach, plan an adventure, schedule an exciting evening out, wait for a birthday, or find a special occasion to experience one another. This is it.

Forget calendars, to-do lists, dirty dishes, overgrown grass, and littered in-boxes.

We surrender to the moment, hold hands, jump in, and swim through the cool, deep waters together...feeling our oneness and the unexplainable mystery of how and why we're together. Without words, we honor the sacredness of this union.

This connection feels ancient...new...difficult...and easy. The hardest thing in the world and the most delicious. Above all, it's unique and it's ours.

When we stop everything. Every. Single. Thing. We find delicious comfort and respite in our three beautiful, interconnected hearts.

We feel the fleeting sweetness of being in each other's presence. We relax. We remember. We breathe out the entire world.

And we know, this, this is all we need. This is all there is.

As I mentioned earlier, one summer I informally surveyed hundreds of families around the United States and Canada on what enhances their sense of harmony, peace, and emotional well-being. Topping the list was spending time together: just being together, consciously connecting.

I met my husband on a hiking expedition to Mexico's Yucatán Peninsula. The group included seventy people from all over the United States and at various life stages, from college kids and New York hippies to retired professionals and young families. Among our traveling troupe was a beautiful, large Mormon family with ten children ages one to sixteen. I'll never forget that family — I loved watching them interact. They were kind, loving, gentle, and respectful to one another; they seemed to enjoy and delight in one another's company. I was intrigued by how they looked each other in the eyes so intently when they spoke. One morning I overheard the mom — who would wake up at 6 A.M. to braid the girls' hair by the campfire while they discussed the upcoming day — talking with another parent in our group. The other parent asked, "How is it that your family seems to get along so well?" The mom responded, "We just really enjoy each other's company — and we choose to spend a lot of time together."

> "It's a mystery how and why we're together — but it's not a mistake. Your family and everything about you is unique — there will never be another tribe just like yours."
> — Renée Trudeau

The family of twelve enjoyed each other so much exactly because they *chose* to spend time together, not the other way around. They got that spending time together was an investment in their family's emotional state and how connected they felt to one another.

How many of us can say the same? It's hard as parents when we're juggling our own needs, work demands, and relationship dynamics to always and fully show up for our families. Many parents wake up on a Monday morning, feel exhausted from an overscheduled weekend, and realize they didn't actually spend that much time together as a family. Or, they were in the *presence* of their family members but weren't truly *present*. Between soccer games, birthday parties, family demands, school projects, and household responsibilities, there can be a lot of shuttling and activity, but few true moments where everyone in the family connects with one another. Or time for the parents to get their own needs met, either.

Consider this: As families, we will spend much more time together as adults than in a parent/child dynamic, so as parents we should ask, "What kind of adult am I raising, and who is this person I'll be hanging out with for the next fifty years?"

BEGIN WHERE YOU ARE

It's 7 A.M. I'm sitting at my computer replying to some timely emails before I help my son find his shoes and water bottle and get out the door for school.

Jonah walks into my upstairs office and sits down in the office chair opposite mine and begins to twirl in circles like a madman while telling me about a really cool skateboard trick he saw Connor, his twelve-year-old idol, perform.

When interruptions like this happen — which is often — I try to stop and explain that I can't give Jonah my full attention until I finish the task I'm doing, but I'd love to meet him downstairs shortly. Or I ask if he can save the story for dinnertime. Sometimes I do this in gentle tones. Sometimes there's a sharpness to my voice I wish wasn't there.

But this morning I stop, look up, acknowledge his earnestness and passion, push my laptop aside, and really see him. For a moment, I jump into his world, imagining how he must have felt watching Connor — wishing his small nine-year-old string-bean body could do the same things this testosterone-flooded big boy can. I can feel how badly he wants me to experience his excitement at witnessing this force of nature. And for a moment, a veil is lifted, and I do.

There are degrees of "presence." And sometimes when I think I'm really listening to my son or husband or loved ones, I'm not.

That morning, before my husband and third-grader zipped off to school in our dusty Volkswagen, my son rolled down the window, and I called out to him from the porch: "Maybe I could get a skateboard and we could try some of those tricks together?" He looked at me funny and said, "Mom, that would be embarrassing." Then after a short pause, he added quietly, hopefully, "Would you really do that?" Yes, Jonah, I would.

Cultivating awareness, being fully present for one another, doesn't mean radically changing our schedules or our lives. It's more about our intention: *How* do we want to be when we are together? Spending time together like you mean it, as this chapter's title says, is about slowing down, becoming more present, and really connecting from the heart with the amazing people you live with — your tribe.

As you explore how you can show up in your family relationships more present and alive, I encourage you to do so with a sense of playfulness. Then focus on these ways of relating:

- CULTIVATE CURIOSITY. Take time to get to know your family members; don't assume you already know everything about them. Crawl into their world and experience what makes them tick. What makes them come alive? Even if you have no interest in what are they "into" right now (whether that's football, Barbies, or the latest pop band) you can show your interest in *them*. If you had to introduce your spouse or children to a relative who has passed, how would you describe them?

- EXAMINE YOUR OWN ASSUMPTIONS. Do you have preconceived ideas about what it's like to raise a two-year-old or a sixteen-year-old? Often, people live up (or down) to our expectations, and we can get stuck in parenting ruts and habitual ways of interacting. The past is past; don't miss opportunities to evolve into new ways of being with one another.

- LISTEN WITHOUT JUDGMENT. Try "dropping history" and listening as if you're hearing this person for the first time (a favorite practice in our home). Keep communication fresh, open, and new.

- PLAY TOGETHER! Schedule time to be together engaged in fun activities. For some families, this is no problem. For others, it doesn't always come naturally and may feel forced at first. Persevere. Be silly and have fun together, which encourages a playful way of relating in general; it can add a beautiful levity and lightness when challenging situations arise. Do what's simple and easy: visit your twelve-year-old's secret underground cave behind your home or simply wrestle on the floor.

- GET ADVICE. Loving families are made, not born. Not sure how your seven-year-old is wired? Finding it hard to communicate with your hormone-addled teenager? To start, pick up a copy of *Nurture by Nature* by Paul Tieger and Barbara Barron-Tieger or *The Five Love Languages* by Gary Chapman.

- EXPRESS APPRECIATION OFTEN. Let your spouse and children know you want to be with them, that you value and appreciate time with them, and that you enjoy spending time together. Let them know how special it is for you.

Spending time together as a family has a profound impact on our children's well-being, yet as kids get older, this becomes harder. Children start to prefer the company of their peers, and this is natural. However, it's important to continue communicating that you *want* to spend time together. Too many parents make the mistake of pulling back as their kids get older; they feel like it's too much trouble to demand family time, or they feel they don't have the right to take their kids away from their friends. But you might be surprised by what your kids really think, as opposed to what they say! I used to get really irritated at my dad in high school when he insisted my brothers and I join the family for a Friday-night dinner at our favorite Mexican restaurant (after which we could meet up with our friends). But deep down I appreciated that he actually wanted to be with me — that he wanted to know me even in my sullen teenage state.

> *"We use humor a lot, emulate what the kids do, and familiarize ourselves with their world — activities, TV shows, songs, how they interact and play. This makes the kids happy and feel like their interests matter."*
> — Andrew, 40, father of two

My good friend Caroline, mom to two teen girls, often shares stories on our lakeside walks about how her daughters are navigating boyfriend dilemmas, body-image questions, finding God, and finding themselves. They're forthcoming and open with her (certainly not like I was with my mom when I was sixteen!). My guess is that Caroline has helped create this openness by making clear she relishes the time with her daughters — but most of all, she listens. A lot. Without judgment. And she makes spending time with them and her whole family a top priority.

CREATING MEANINGFUL FAMILY TIME

In junior high I often visited my friend Kim's house, and I don't recall a single time when her parents and teenage brother were not all yelling at one another. It's like they were preparing for a play, and they were constantly rehearsing the "fight scene."

Maybe family time at your house is less than ideal. You may have gotten stuck in a pattern of arguing, retreating to separate rooms, and checking out by plugging into media, or maybe one parent is frequently gone, so just gathering can be a feat unto itself?! Where to start? With baby steps and a lot of self-compassion. Just keep it simple, begin — and acknowledge — where you are, and build from there. Consider the following ideas for creating meaningful connections with your family:

- CREATE SOME SHORT, SIMPLE RITUALS. During those moments when the family is all together naturally — during meals, at bedtime, first thing in the morning — create little rituals to remind everyone to see and really connect with each other. In our house, before each meal, we say "eyes" and take a moment to look each other in the eyes; yes, my son thinks this is kooky, but he's gotten used to it! This "ritual" could be as simple as giving long hugs before each person leaves for the day, having a midday check-in to *really* hear how each person's day is going, or sharing a heartfelt "I love you" at night.

- SCHEDULE FAMILY DINNERS TOGETHER. Treat family dinners like any other important commitment and schedule them on set evenings. You may need to get creative if your schedules are erratic: Mom has dinner with one child earlier and Dad has dinner with another child later, or Tuesdays and Thursdays are family dinner nights.

- EACH DAY, HAVE EACH FAMILY MEMBER SHARE ABOUT THEIR DAY. During dinner or at bedtime, make sure everyone has a chance to talk about what they did and how they feel. This could be as simple as asking for a "thumbs-up" or a "thumbs-down" where everyone shares their highs and lows for the day. Even teenagers seem to respond to this wording.

- TRY "10-ON-10S." This was a popular term in the 1970s in marriage counseling; it referred to having Mom and Dad spend ten minutes right after work decompressing and sharing about their day. But it's still a great idea, and it works for the whole family. Ellen, a single mom, has "10-on-10s" and snacks with her two young sons right when they walk in the door from school. It's a great way to connect and shift gears before dinner. Her boys love it!

- ONCE A WEEK, GET TOGETHER UNPLUGGED. Make sure that every week, for an afternoon, evening, or whole day, your entire family gathers to relax and have fun as a group. As with dinners, schedule this time ahead. Most of all, turn off the TV and iPad; family time unplugged can be a catalyst for all kinds of adventures and new ways to be together.

- PLAN FAMILY DATE NIGHTS. Schedule an evening once a month for an extraspecial family fun night. Get the entire family's input on what they want to do, and try to make it unusual or out of the ordinary: perhaps dim sum and bowling, a picnic outdoors and stargazing, going to a major art museum, or preparing a unique gourmet feast at home.

- SYNC UP EVERYONE'S CALENDAR EACH MONTH. Don't leave family time to chance. Sit everyone down together with their calendars, go over the month's activities, and make sure family time is scheduled like every other commitment. This usually means making hard choices — perhaps canceling some activities or saying no — but it's worth it. It also sends the message to everyone in your tribe that family comes first.

- INTRODUCE OR BRING BACK A BELOVED BEDTIME RITUAL. I know some families that still read to their kids at night before bed, and their children are sixteen! If you've fallen out of this routine, bring it back, or introduce a new communal family bedtime ritual: snuggle in Mom and Dad's bed or on the couch, read out loud a book you all enjoy, do round-robin storytelling, or share back or foot massages.

- GET CREATIVE WITH FAMILY TRIPS. Of course, taking yearly, extended family vacations ensures quality time together, but these aren't always possible, so think outside the box. Instead, plan separate, shorter, mother/daughter and father/son vacations. Plan a series of day trips to unusual spots. If parents travel, plan for group Skype calls. If your kids have left the nest, maybe organize a weekend family reunion.

- SCHEDULE REGULAR FAMILY MEETINGS. These could be monthly, quarterly, or as needed, but they would be expressly for taking care of family "business": to share important news, resolve issues, discuss disagreements, or plan for upcoming events. Let all family members propose agenda items (keep a running list on the fridge), ask that everyone come with an open heart (we like to sit on the floor in a circle), listen as much as you talk, set a time limit for the meeting, start with a kudos for each person, and encourage problem solving and brainstorming. Having a "talking stick" can help avoid interruptions so everyone is heard.

- CREATE A FAMILY VISION BOARD. These are great ways for everyone to express and share their dreams and desires. Have each person brainstorm and choose three words and some corresponding images from a magazine that represent the kind of year (or upcoming season) he or she would like to have. Everyone takes turns sharing what they chose, and why. Then paste or tape all the words and images on a large piece of paper for display in a prominent place.

What ideas come to mind as you contemplate consciously scheduling family time to be together? What are ways you already enjoy being together? What are things you used to do as a family, or that you once did as a young child, that you may want to reintroduce? Make this easy and work for you — so it will stick.

As you consider these things and develop new habits and routines, keep a few things in mind. First of all, acknowledge that it will take work. I know how difficult it can be creating space for family time. Everyone has their own particular challenges, whether that's a single-parent household, one parent who travels a lot for work, a merged family, a very large family, or a child with special needs. For any family, it will take a high level of commitment and a certain level of vigilance. This is why consciously planning ahead for family time is critical.

Then, during those weeks when it feels like you're moving mountains, remember what a huge impact time together makes on your family's well-being. In my family, everyone's week is significantly improved when we create space — during the week and weekend — to ground with each other through meaningful activities and time together. Isn't it wonderful when you feel anchored with those you love most? Wouldn't it be great to create this all the time, every day? To feel emotional support flowing between you and the sense that your family has your back? You can and you will. As you stick with it, you'll discover what the Mormon mom shared: the more time families spend together, the more time they *want* to be together. When we relate to each other on a deeper level, this time together nourishes us and we begin to long for it.

Finally, remember that it's all about balance. We can't do everything all the time. Adopting a "good is good enough" mindset helps. Some weeks we may have less family time than we want if we have a big deadline at work, and other weeks we may get less done on the home or professional front if we're spending more time with our family. For myself, I always have to watch for my perfectionist, controlling side. When I let go of rigidity, the need to hold it together, or my expectations of how things should be, my time with my family flows.

For instance, when my son was a baby, I was in a weekly play group with a wonderful group of women. While I love a clean house as much as the next person, my friend Paula and I used to joke, "Dust bunnies be damned!" We were both raised by artist mothers who believed that playing, painting, cooking, creating, and connecting with those we loved would always trump a clean house, and our homes could never pass a white-glove test. I'm still this way…most of the time. But sometimes I wake up on a Saturday morning in Helen Housecleaner mode, and I realize that, to create calm in our family's hearts and minds, we need to spend some time clearing clutter and bringing order to our home space. Working together can also be family time.

There is so much joy, learning, growth, and new perspectives available to us when we begin to really slow down, be more present, and fully show up to and for our family members. As you spend more time together as a family, you'll be amazed by all the good that's right there in front of you.

CONNECTING with YOUR PARTNER

If it's hard enough creating family time, it can feel impossible making couples time with your spouse. Remember when you used to do that?

However, when Mom and Dad are connected, family time flows more naturally for everyone. When you experience time together as a couple away from the kids — when you and your partner feel connected and on the same team — you're able to be more generous in heart and spirit with your children. Harmony begins with you.

Notice how your kids respond when you and your spouse display love and affection toward each other. Happiness is contagious. I have a strong memory of feeling warmth and love spreading through my body when I would see my dad put his arms around my mom and hold her.

Here are a few ways to stay connected to your partner as you navigate everyday life:

- SCHEDULE TIME FOR YOUR NEEDS FIRST. Block out time for self-renewal just like you would schedule a dentist's appointment. One night a week schedule a "solo date," or time alone getting your needs met, whether that's dinner with a friend or attending a yoga class alone. Then you'll be able to fully enjoy and feel more generous and loving during your time with your spouse.
- USE THE POWER OF TOUCH. Make a habit to stay physically connected to your partner whenever you see him or her in thoughtful, easy ways: hugs and kisses in the morning and at the end of the day, quick neck or shoulder massages, gentle arm touches, holding hands. Physicality increases our emotional connection.
- COMMUNICATE RESPECTFULLY AND MANAGE YOUR OWN FRUSTRATIONS. Partners don't always agree. That's okay, but when our emotions get heated, we can say and do things we later regret. Recognize your limits, and when you are about to blow, take action first:

my husband and I often resort to "quiet breaks" when we reach this point. Also, be mindful of what you know triggers or upsets your partner and avoid it.

- WRITE AN INTENTION STATEMENT FOR YOUR PARTNERSHIP. This can be a powerful way to communicate what you want your relationship to represent: Is your focus mutual support, spiritual growth, honesty and communication, love and respect? Frame your statement and place it in your bedroom in a visible spot.
- SHARE THE BIG PICTURE AND COMMUNICATE OFTEN. Make sure your partner knows what's going on with you on all fronts by telling him or her. If you have a particularly challenging day or week ahead, and you may need some extra support and TLC, give your partner a heads-up.
- ENSURE YOUR BEDROOM REFLECTS YOUR MARRIAGE. A feng shui consultant once asked me, "Why do you have all this artwork of women up in your bedroom? Where are the pictures of you and your husband?" Great point. Carefully choose for your bedroom items you love and cherish that celebrate your union: special photos of you and your partner, meaningful artwork, candles, a marriage intention statement, and so on. My husband and I created a small "marriage altar" in our bedroom that has our wedding candle and love letters we've written to each other. Also, try to keep your bedroom a toy-free zone. Make it a space solely for relaxation, intimacy, sleep, and connection.
- EVERY DAY, TALK, SHARE, CONNECT, AND STATE YOUR NEEDS. At a minimum, take ten minutes at the end of each day (after the kids are in bed) to take turns sharing the highs and lows of your day, anticipating tomorrow, and asking for what you might need. Saying "Three things I need from our relationship now are..." is a simple but powerful request. Your needs will change depending on the time of the year, your life stage, and your kids' ages. For more about this type of sharing, see *Love Tune-Ups* by Matthew McKay, Carole Honeychurch, and Angela Watrous. This is a quick but really effective way to reconnect. Or try Tanya's strategy; she shares: "We like to take long, hot baths together after the kids are in bed — try staying mad when you're covered in bubbles!"

THE GIFT of BEING SEEN

Spiritual teacher Eckhart Tolle says one of the biggest gifts we can give our children is not stuff or vacations but to really see them — to be with them. He shares in his book *A New Earth*, "Many children harbor hidden anger and resentment toward their parents and often the cause is inauthenticity in the relationship. The child has a deep longing for the parent to be there as a human being, not as a role, no matter how conscientiously that role is being played. You may be doing all the right things and the best you can for your child, but...doing is never enough if you neglect Being."

One morning when I was ten, I walked into our big open kitchen and my eyes were drawn to four tiny green baskets sitting on the yellow Formica countertop next to my mom's glass jars of grains and legumes. In my basket was a purple bottle of bubbles, some Wacky Packs (my favorite), healthy rice crispy cookies, and pink barrettes. My mom stood quietly — baby on hip, cloaked in remorse for having withdrawn and mostly ignored us due to a black cloud of depression that had settled over her the previous week — and said, "I'm sorry." Uncomfortable and unable to look at one another, my three brothers and I dove into our basket of treats. We were all feeling sad, but we were too young and too confused to know how to respond or ask for what we really needed.

I was moved by her loving gesture, but in that moment, all I really wanted was for my mom to gather us in her arms and share from her heart why she had disappeared and to know that I was loved. I didn't want stuff. I wanted her to drop everything and be with me.

My friend Sara Hickman is a talented musician, artist, and peace activist, and she wrote a moving song about being present with our kids. On her album *Big Kids*, her daughter Lily (then six years old) sings the following song (which was also performed on the 2004 season of *American Idol*).

"Look at Me" by Sara Hickman

Put down the paper
Hang up the phone

Please see me as more than a dog
That you throw a bone
Let's go for a walk
Yea, let's go outside
No I don't want to hop in the car
And go for a ride
I need a genuine encounter
Of the first degree
I need you to stop what you're doing
And look at me...look at me
Look at me look at me look at me look at me
    now!
You're awfully busy
Got things to do
Just give me a moment of time
With you
I've got all these ideas I want you to see
There's a person who's growing up
Inside of me
I need your full attention
And I deserve it, too
I'm somebody important
I'm a part of you
A part of you
Look at me look at me look at me look at me
Please don't be angry
I'm just a kid
I'm only doing the things
That you once did

Of course, all of us need to be seen and heard — adults do, too. But the difference is that adults can often wait for an appropriate time and defer their needs, and children can't. They live in the moment, and they need our attention now!

And what a difference it makes when we do honor our children, when we see and celebrate them for who they are right now. My son's school has a ritual of honoring each child on his or her birthday with a song circle and accolades from classmates, and when my son turned eight, my husband and I attended his class birthday circle.

It was an amazing experience. How often do any of us get the opportunity to hear from our closest friends and family what they love and honor about us? In keeping with this, every year I now write a birthday letter to my son about his current stage — what he loves, what's going on in his world at the time, and what I love about him. Then I usually read my letter at our extended-family birthday dinner. It's important that our kids know that who they are will always be more important than what they do. That they're "enough" just as they are.

> *"We create little pockets of time to connect: sharing 'highlights' and 'low lights' during dinner and spending five to ten unrushed minutes at bedtime to let the kids talk about whatever they want while we just listen."*
> — Amy, 41, mother of three

Jonah's birthday celebration ended with the "Star Song." This song — sung at every child's birthday — always brings me to tears: "Jonah, Jonah, you shine like a star. I love you, Jonah, just as you are." Couldn't we all use a daily dose of that?

THE GIFT of NOW

One morning I went to wake up my little guy, and I found him curled up tightly in his blue-and-green dragon comforter — a small sleeping cocoon. Sitting next to him in the dark, I gently rubbed his back. I pushed his hair off his face and kissed his sweet chubby cheeks. He smiled. I let him know there was no rush; he could wake up slowly.

Thirty minutes later while he was eating his breakfast, he told me how much he liked the way I woke him up. He said, "We all need to slow down, Mom. It's better that way. That's how we're supposed to live."

What is the pace of your life, and of your thoughts, right now? Is it the pace you prefer, one that allows you to be present in the moment, or are you letting others or your environment set the pace for you? It's not about being critical; there are times to move fast and times to move slow. But are we living mindfully, cultivating awareness, and moving at a pace that allows us to be fully present for one another?

Tapping the "power of slow" and consciously choosing to slow down and live more in the present moment is a great way to practice self-care, and it also enhances our connection to others. When my thoughts are racing, I'm somewhere else. My young son nailed it when he said we need to slow down. It's how we're supposed to live. Right here, right now.

For instance, my favorite hike and bike trail wraps around a beautiful lake and runs through the center of downtown Austin. I typically take this walk with a friend, but one day I found myself craving my own sweet, silent company. As I walked the trail, I felt the gravel crunch under my Keens, dryness in my mouth, and sweat running down my back and the back of my arms. I've done this walk easily a hundred times. How many times had my mind been somewhere else — anticipating the next approaching landmark, what kind of taco I was going to eat for breakfast, my growing to-do list awaiting me back at the office? This time I slowed down — not my pace but my mind. I allowed myself to come fully into the present moment. I noticed the smells and sights around me as if for the first time: strong body odor, rotting plants, sweet honeysuckle, and how the brilliant Technicolor flowering crepe myrtle trees that lined the path seemed to explode before my eyes. At one point, I had to stop to take in the beauty of the cactus blooms — their intensity was so overwhelming.

I also became more aware of my own body: the slightly metallic taste in my mouth, my breathing, my leg muscles, and how everything worked together in harmony to effortlessly carry me the 3.6-mile distance around the lake. Nothing was any different from any other day, and yet the experience was transformed simply through awareness. I had to wonder: How many times had I missed moments, words, facial expressions, subtle nuances in communication? How many times had I missed opportunities to connect — never-to-be-repeated moments — with those I love most simply from not being fully present? From waking up too fast and being in too much of a hurry to get up, get going, and get everything done?

I'm sure you've experienced moments like this, when you've awakened and tried to carry that sense of presence with you throughout your day. But it's challenging. It's easy to engage our "monkey mind" and find ways to avoid showing up fully. When you're feeling scattered and finding it hard to "be here now" in your relationships, try pausing and asking the following questions:

- In this moment and this interaction, am I living in the past, present, or future? (Stress and anxiety are signals we're living in either the past or the future. There is no stress if we're fully engaged in the present moment.)
- In this moment, what is most important to me?
- Does this activity really have to get accomplished today, right now?
- If there's a problem, ask yourself: In a year from now, will this chore, argument, or event really matter?

Around our home, we often remind each other, "Relationships first, things second." Our time on planet Earth is short. You never know if the conversation you have with a family member or friend today might be your last.

After I had delivered a keynote speech entitled "Saying Yes to Your Calling," a woman in her midforties came up to me with tears streaming down her face. She said that she realized for the first time that she has not been present in her own life. Present for herself. She was crying, she said, because she wondered what she had missed.

In our wise moments, we know that at the end of our lives, we won't lament not having washed the car, cleaned out the gutters, or painted the house. But if we're not mindful and fully present to ourselves and others now, we might mourn the loss of not drinking in a big full moon in a dark night sky with someone we love, the deliciously unmistakable smell of a baby's head, the fresh feel of an early-morning bike ride with our child, or allowing our hearts to fully open to those who sleep under the same roof with us every night.

"Sometimes we save ourselves for life's special moments — birthdays, graduations, promotions, weddings, vacations, special celebrations. But we don't need to. Showing up and expressing ourselves fully can be part of our everyday experience."
— Renée Trudeau

FAMILY TIME IS SACRED

One Saturday, I had a particularly full schedule. As I moved from task to task — farmer's market, yoga, picking up supplies for my son's school project, a store return — I felt my heart soften and open, and I was hit with a wave of longing to be with my partner and son.

I dropped my to-do list and headed home. The guys were vacuuming the living room, making popcorn, and sorting laundry, and they were surprised when I called them over to join me on the floor in our living room. I reached out for a family hug and told them how much I love them and enjoy being with them and that there's nothing more important than being together like this. We ended up having a family wrestle (my son's favorite), left the housework to wait, and went for a walk and then to a Chinese restaurant for lunch.

Family time is sacred. Protect your time together — and grab moments to celebrate it whenever you can, whenever inspiration strikes or your intuition nudges you. Sometimes we save ourselves for life's special moments — birthdays, graduations, promotions, weddings, vacations, special celebrations. But we don't need to. Showing up and expressing ourselves fully can be part of our everyday experience. Heartfelt connection can happen every time we get together. Everyone in our family deserves our full attention — all the time, not just some of the time.

What kind words, thoughtful gestures, caring actions, or fun activities are you saving for a special time or place? Why not share these with your children and family right now?

As I was working on this book, I asked Jonah, who was then nine: If he had just one thing to tell parents about what their kids want, what would he share? He paused, then replied, "Mom, tell them to surprise their kids, to have fun with them, to listen to them. And really, to just spend time with them."

Pat on the Back

WHAT'S WORKING?

What is one thing you currently do — or have done in the past — to make spending time together with your family a priority?

Putting It into Practice

MEETING EACH OTHER...AGAIN

Often we think we know our family members better than we actually do. Set up a family date to get to know one another. Make it fun and light, and take turns asking each other personal (but age-appropriate) questions. How present can you be with one another? Allow yourself to be surprised. Don't assume you know everyone's answers. Honor what's being shared. When you're done, have everyone share what they learned from this exercise. Here are some possible questions to get you started:

- What surprised you?
- What quality do you want to come to mind when people think of you?
- If you could design your ideal day, what would it look like?
- If you had to live on two foods for a week, what would they be?
- What makes your heart sad? What makes you cry?

Imagine a New Way of Being

A JOURNALING EXERCISE

Close your eyes for a minute and place one hand over the center of your chest. Take a deep breath. Observe with curiosity and compassion whatever thoughts and feelings this chapter has stirred up for you. When you're ready, explore the following:

- What would it look like for you to spend more dedicated time with family each week?
- How would it feel to spend more time with your family?
- How might your relationships or family life shift if you started spending more time together?

PAUSE for PEACE
Quickie Journaling

If you're new to journaling and unsure how to start, or you
feel like you don't have the time for this practice, play with what I
call "quickie journaling": take five minutes to answer three questions.
This is easy to do almost anywhere and anytime that fits your schedule:
at your desk before you start work, in your car in between drop-offs and
errands, before bedtime — and it's amazingly powerful. Buy a journal
— or a grocery-store notebook — and once a day for a week respond to
the following three questions: How do I feel? What do I need? What do I
want? Write from your gut — without overanalyzing. Write the first thing
that comes to mind using stream-of-consciousness writing, pausing
between questions. Come from your heart and just let your responses
pour out. This process of inquiry helps us tune in and honor our
needs, and the more you do it, the easier it gets. It's an easy
way to begin cultivating your inner world — which is
as important as, or more important than, your
outer world.

Chapter 7

DEFINING, CELEBRATING, and HONORING YOUR FAMILY CULTURE

In the early 1980s, after our six-year sojourn living in Northern California, my adventurous parents moved us back to Texas to an ultraconservative, upper-middle-class community in San Antonio. They explained to us that we were moving back because of the increased number of school options in Texas, but I think that knowing how many of our California teachers grew their own marijuana supply became too much for them. I don't think my parents fully realized what a culture clash we would encounter in Texas, going from a community of seekers to a community of socialites. We could not have stuck out more — from our Birkenstocks, Hang Ten clothing, vegetarian diet, and VW van to our anticonsumerism views. At our new school, my siblings and I understood immediately that our family differed from everyone else, but we couldn't have articulated why. We felt lost, unsure of who we were, in part because my parents didn't sit us down beforehand and discuss our family's values and how this new world might differ.

Each family has its own personality, which is a reflection of its shared values. These are the attitudes and attributes it considers most important. As parents, we establish our family's values and priorities, but our children also have voices and opinions of their own, particularly as they get older. Thus, it's important both to articulate your family's values and to create a safe container where everyone can express their opinions and self. Our families should be our sanctuaries. A place where we can show up warts and all. Ideally, we can create a safe haven where each family member can be fully heard and seen and respected, and where they can find comfort, support, and respite. As families, we help each other discover and remember who we really are and what really matters. Too often, child development expert and author Gordon Neufeld says, "we make children work for our love instead of resting in it." As was the case in my family growing up, this sort of big-picture, values-based sharing often gets lost and overlooked in the course of our daily lives. Yet it's essential if we're to survive and thrive.

DEFINING YOUR CULTURE: WHAT DO YOU STAND FOR?

One Saturday our entire family was in total disequilibrium. Gripped by a sudden inspiration, I gathered oversized paper and markers and asked my husband and son to join me on the floor in front of our fireplace. They weren't too thrilled — sighs and rolling eyes abounded — but eventually they made their way to the living room.

I said I wanted to brainstorm together the top three qualities we wanted to honor in our family — a kind of manifesto. What did we stand for? What was our family culture — our values? At first, we each created our own list, which we then shared. After some spirited group discussion and negotiation, we came up with a list of five qualities we all agreed on.

What does your family value the most? At the end of the day, what's most important to you? Look around your home: What does your environment say about what you most value?

We may know what we value individually, but have we expressed a collective purpose and shared values as a family? Your family household includes some of the most important people in your life: Where are you going day to day? What are you trying to accomplish and embody?

At the end of this chapter is an exercise for creating your family values statement. For now, as a start, consider this list of qualities, themes, and attributes. Which speak to you as the most important for your family? What would you add — based on any cultural or religious traditions you follow — to this list?

- love
- listening and understanding
- creativity
- openhearted communication
- support
- playfulness and humor
- new experiences and adventure
- hard work
- respect
- service to others and volunteering
- open-mindedness
- kindness and compassion
- experiencing nature and preserving it
- accountability
- fiscal responsibility
- social and/or political activism
- healthy diet and lifestyle
- physical fitness and sports
- cultural arts and music

That Saturday afternoon at our house, after discussing and integrating everyone's individual values, we came up with the following family values statement and posted it on our fireplace mantle.

Trudeau Family Values:
Creativity
Openhearted Communication
Loving Support

Playfulness
Health and Vitality

When the time comes, have fun with this conversation; keep it light. Approach the idea of defining your family culture with a lot of curiosity, a positive mindset, and a sense of humor. One of my friends joked that her entire family was so obsessed with the Wii that their culture could pretty much be summed up as "Wii are family!" One of the gifts that can come from this dialogue is seeing to what degree your current lifestyle and home are actually aligned with your values. This discussion can make the perfect moment to rethink and redefine your priorities and how you do things. You're in the driver's seat. You can change how you interact with each other and start fresh anytime — it's refreshing and exhilarating!

Our family values creativity and playfulness, and we transformed the living room in our house, which is the first room you enter from our front door, into our "creativity room" — it's now a large, open space free of furniture except for oversized orange and aqua pillows stacked in the corner, artwork and photography on the walls, and a piano and percussion instruments. This space was designed solely for dancing and movement, music making, creative play, and pillow fights! In this way, our home embodies our values — plus, whenever disequilibrium strikes again, this is the go-to room when Jonah and I need to "shake it off."

EXPLORING WHAT MATTERS to YOU

I grew up in a family of overachievers. As the oldest, it was not easy to ignore the pervasive "in our family we make A grades" theme song that echoed throughout the halls of our home. My parents valued creativity and self-expression, but they also made it very clear that if you were going to dance, you better be closing in on Mikhail Baryshnikov (a slight exaggeration). Expectations were high in the Peterson household. This value — even if it wasn't specifically vocalized — had a big impact on me when I was young. I tried and then abandoned many sports and activities — ballet, tennis, violin, singing, and more — whenever I deemed I wasn't superior. I figured, "Why try? Stick to what you really excel at." One of my younger brothers played the violin from the age of five. As he grew, so did the pressure to excel and become the next Itzhak Perlman. At some point, it stopped being fun for him, and my brother decided to drop it his freshman year in high school. Today, he regrets that our family circumstances didn't support a different outcome.

These experiences left me wanting to create a different relationship for my child regarding competition and achievement. One Saturday morning when my husband, son, and I were out exploring, we stumbled across a national rowing competition on the lake. High school and college kids — and their families and friends — from around the United States were clumped in camps up and down the lakeside, surrounded by their long skinny boats. You could feel the excitement, tension, and pressure in the air — they were there to win! The race — in all of its glorious hypercompetitiveness — gave us the perfect segue to explore this topic with my son over lunch.

Competition can be healthy, and it is very American. The problem with this "if you're going to play, you need to be the best" philosophy is that you miss out on a lot of things that you might actually want to do just for fun. Just for the pure joy of the activity — regardless of your ability.

"Are you living the life you desire, or someone else's entirely?"
— Renée Trudeau

I thought how much I want to impart this mindset to my son.

I recently took an intuitive painting class that challenged the students to paint without a goal in mind. Paint what you feel in the moment. Don't try to be good or make your painting look pretty. Just enjoy the diversity and vibrancy of the colors, the brushstrokes, how the images make you feel, how much fun it is to do something with no desired outcome. I want our family culture to embrace the belief that there are many cool things we'll want to try in life, and that we don't have to excel at them to enjoy them. There is no scorecard for happiness or for the excitement that comes from trying new things.

Reflect for a moment on what values were key to your family of origin (whether they were articulated or not): What experiences did you have growing up that affected what values you see as important today? What are values you desire to teach your child about and to honor and celebrate with your family? Have you discussed these with your partner, and are you on the same page regarding what is most important to you individually and as a family? Are you living the life you desire, or someone else's entirely?

PARENTS on the SAME PAGE

Discussing family values is a conversation for the whole family. But it's also true that, as parents, spouses or partners need to be in agreement with each other. Exploring this is sometimes best handled as a separate conversation.

One morning after my son had gone to school, my husband, who had been recently laid off from his tech job, and I took an early-morning walk together. Initially, we were just trying to get caught up on our schedules, but soon we realized we weren't really synced up on *big* life stuff and where we were headed as a couple and a family. We try to regularly schedule time for date nights, meditate together most mornings, and visit in the evenings after dinner, but here we were both at major life junctures, and we weren't harnessing or leveraging our collective power, intention, and strengths. It was as if we had both been hiking in the woods — intersecting at rest stops — but neither of us had met the other on the mountaintop in quite some time.

Inspired, we canceled all of our meetings and plans for the following Friday and scheduled our own personal five-hour visioning retreat. Together, we wanted to focus on our careers, how we want to share our talents with the world, and our highest vision for our lives. We meditated and prayed together, tapped inspirational readings, listed and voiced our talents, created vision boards, and shared what we desire for our family. We enjoyed some yoga and stretching, and we finished with a walk to visit my parents' memorial bench, where we did a gratitude sharing.

The retreat gave us the chance to align on a much higher level than we ever get to do on a day-to-day basis. The break also helped us get clear on what was important to us as a family.

If we're not on the same page with our partner about what's most important to us as a couple and a family, how can we expect our children to be on board? (For more tips on staying connected to your partner, see chapter 6, page 109.)

HONORING YOUR FAMILY CULTURE: NEXT STEPS

Once you've clarified who you are — and who you want to be — as a family, it's time to figure out how to embody or manifest those attributes in your day-to-day life. This will look different for everyone, but it could involve changing the "extracurricular" activities people are involved in, establishing media guidelines or new ways family members interact with each other, shifting your diet and/or how often you move your bodies, redecorating or repurposing rooms in your house, and scheduling more and various kinds of family time.

As you get down to specifics, try to avoid lists of "rules." As parents, we want to exert control, but this isn't an opportunity to micromanage family members — who wants to do that?! Instead, respect and allow for differences, and seek solutions that honor what matters to everyone without pushing people's buttons or creating guidelines that feel "punitive." It's key to get clear on your values and then find ways to celebrate and support them in your day-to-day choices. When approached in this positive way, it's easier for everyone to buy in to choices.

Another key is to identify what I call "nonnegotiables." Nonnegotiables are your family's absolutes — the rules everyone agrees to without exception (one of ours is speaking to one another with love and respect).

Some major nonnegotiable arenas include:

- MEDIA GUIDELINES. Will you establish media-free family dinners, or rules for when, where, and for how long playing video games or TV watching is allowed?
- FOOD AND MEALS. Will you establish regular family dinner nights? Will you make changes to the family diet and what you eat? Should cooking and shopping be shared or rotated among family members? How often will the family eat out or order in (if at all)?
- DATE NIGHTS AND FAMILY ACTIVITIES. Does everyone have the

time they want and need to do what they enjoy, alone and together? Will Mom and Dad plan a monthly date night? Does the family have regular togetherness time, or a weekly day of rest (like a Sunday Sabbath)?

- FAMILY MEETINGS. Should the family have weekly or monthly gatherings to go over important family news, scheduling, or issues that need addressing? If yes, what will these look like, and can anyone call a meeting at any time?

- COMMUNICATION GUIDELINES. What's the expectation for handling disagreements? Does everyone have the same definition for what behavior reflects kindness and respect? What strategies or practices will you tap to enhance listening and clear communication with one another?

After you've sorted through and identified your family's nonnegotiables, consider creating some kind of ritual to enliven these and embed them into your daily life. Perhaps you draw up a family contract and go over these at a family meeting (and have each member sign) — or do something more informal, such as reviewing these over dessert one evening after dinner.

"Creating rituals and sticking to them is important to us: family date night, Saturdays with Dad, nightly story time, and a daily thirty-minute play date with my daughter, where she chooses what we do. My goal is to be fully present with her."
— Rebecca, 44, mother of two

Getting really clear on our values — and having all our key decisions based on these — can bring the sense of freedom, peace, and calm to our routines that many of us have been craving. And these values can serve as a guiding force for all areas of our lives.

THE COURAGE to TAKE a STAND

When my family moved from California back to Texas, I learned firsthand what it meant to stand out from the crowd. When my girlfriends came over to our house, they were fed vegetarian food for dinner, the living room lacked a TV, a life-size fourteenth-century manger scene occupied our dining area, and musical instruments lived in almost every room in our house. It was evident our family was different. When we're with peer groups, it's so easy to succumb to what everyone else is doing. Who hasn't been at a birthday party and said yes to their child's request for a second cupcake when they normally would have said no — simply because everyone else was having one?

Last year I attended a screening for Vicki Abeles's documentary *Race to Nowhere*, a powerful look at how our current education model and drive for achievement are negatively affecting our kids. After the film, they held a question-and-answer session exploring what we can do to challenge and improve our current school system, and a mother of three stood up. She shared that during her daughter's first week of public school, she went into the principal's office and kindly but firmly said, "Hi, I'm Susan Neptune. You'll probably remember my name because my daughter, Erin, who is in first grade, will not be doing any homework. I feel her afternoons are best served by playing in the creek behind our house."

While you may have a different opinion about homework, I wanted to stand up, cheer, and applaud this mother for being so clear on her family's values and for her courage and unwavering commitment to what works — and doesn't work — for them.

If your family had a mantra, what would it be?

Taking a stand for your beliefs requires courage — a willingness to take the road less traveled and to stand out from the crowd. Other people, and certainly your own children, may not agree with your choices, but by sticking to them, you demonstrate the importance of your values.

In the eighth grade, I was mortified when my father came and picked me up in the middle of a sleepover party and took me home while my girlfriends went out to our local movie theater to see the just-released, R-rated film *Saturday Night Fever*. Understandably, he didn't feel an R-rated movie was appropriate for a junior high girl. After the movie, he brought me back to the party, where we stayed up late eating popcorn and singing Bee Gees tunes at the top of our lungs. As angry as I was at the time (and embarrassed, since I was the only girl whose parents didn't think this movie was okay for a fourteen-year-old), another part of me was relieved that my dad would step in to help guide me as I navigated these important times and that he cared enough to protect my innocence for a little while longer.

My friend Ellen recently told me, "Our friends in Minneapolis go to their family cabin every other weekend. This means they miss soccer games, birthday and school events, and Sunday church service two weekends a month. For some, this may seem outlandish. To me, it's incredible. That is dedicated time the whole family *knows* they'll be spending together and away from the rat race of school and extracurricular activities! She inspired me to plan family camping trips once a month in the fall and spring, two of the most hectic times of the year."

It's hard to take a stand for what's important to you. There are times we'll have to step up and stand out — even like a sore thumb — for not following the herd. More often, we will face many smaller moments throughout each day when we have to make choices that reflect what we value. But first we have to know what our values are.

WE ARE FAMILY: CELEBRATING YOUR FAMILY CULTURE

One sunny afternoon in the 1970s, my mom, dad, brother, and I were having a discussion about the presidential campaign. I remember my parents passionately saying, "Well, in our family we believe in supporting welfare and helping people going through hard times, so we're going to vote for XYZ."

Even though I was only ten, this moment really stayed with me. I liked the fact that although my parents encouraged us to be free thinkers, they were communicating what our family valued, what mattered to us. What was essential to the fabric of our beliefs.

Around our household, we constantly say, "Well, in our family we believe...and everyone's family is different." I'm sure my son gets tired of hearing this in response to why he can't have the latest electronic gadget, but I also think hearing this anchors him. Kids want to know where you stand on important issues and what your family values. It gives them a sense of pride to be able to articulate what their family stands for. This will also help them as they get older, enter adolescence, and explore beliefs that are contrary to yours, for they will already know how to articulate and stand up for their values!

This is about more than just taking stands, however. It's about the family providing unconditional love and emotional support for one another when people need it. One morning before my husband had a particularly important meeting at work, I pulled my family together in the living room, and we instituted what we now call "Family Power Circles." When someone is facing a challenge, we wrap our arms around each other's waists, put our heads together, take some deep breaths, acknowledge the support in our lives, say a prayer, and verbally shower the person who needs our blessings with power qualities: courage, trust, strength, wisdom. Then we send the person out the door and into the world.

People first and things second. That's the most essential value. In a family, no one rows out to sea alone, braving the cold, choppy waters all by themselves; we are interdependent and interconnected. Like your grandma's worn pink-and-blue hand-crocheted blanket, a family is woven together through decades of births, deaths, and transitions. There's a reason you're with these people. Open your heart and let them in. Together, identify, choose, and stand up for the life you desire. Stand up for your family.

> "My husband often says to our family, 'United we stand, people!' It may sound goofy, but it often helps remind us that we are all on the same team — we're rooting for, not opposing, one another!"
> — Gina, 39, mother of three

And have serious fun doing so. For instance, if you had a family mascot, what would it be? What would be your family's theme song, your logo? If your family were on a TV sitcom, which actors would play you? Find playful ways to embody your family's personality and cultivate a sense of group identity. What's your family's favorite meal? What's your favorite group activity or card game? What's your favorite vacation destination? What's an ideal Sunday afternoon — playing checkers, hiking, bowling, reading, napping on the couch? Do these things. Celebrate and honor who you are and what's important to you.

One of my favorite songs when I was a kid was "The Marvelous Toy" by Peter, Paul, and Mary. I loved the feeling of wonder and joy it evoked. My brothers and I would dance and act out this song over and over again. My son now has this CD, and listening to this song recently inspired an evening of silliness, dancing, and pillow fights, and it brought back a flood of memories of how often a sense of playfulness was present in my home growing up. It's important to me to continue to celebrate these same qualities in my family today.

Whether you're silly, serious, sporty, creative, zany, or intense, there's only one family just like yours. Celebrate your uniqueness and enjoy this gift of one another.

Pat on the Back

WHAT'S WORKING?

What is one thing you do — or have done in the past — to honor and celebrate your family's values or culture?

Putting It into Practice

CREATE A FAMILY VALUES STATEMENT

Set aside an hour for a family meeting dedicated to creating a family values statement. If your children are at least seven — or are mature enough to sit still for a while — they're ready to be an active part of this process. Have family members brainstorm on their own what they consider their top three to five family values; consult and share this chapter's list of values for ideas. Then have each person share his or her choices with the group. Then, working together, create a final list of the three to six values that are most important to everyone. Make sure everyone has a voice in the discussion; it's important that everyone feels heard and that the final list, and the wording of the statement, reflects the family's consensus. However, how you handle this process depends on the size of your family and ages of your kids. Try to include the input and participation of everyone, even very young kids who cannot yet write, but of course use your judgment. Not everyone may be able to participate equally. Once it's finished, post this values statement where everyone can see it. Make copies for each family member's room. If you like, decorate or color your list; make it into a display or art piece. Perhaps even brainstorm an image, mascot, or design that represents your family values; create a family logo or crest.

The list should feel like you. It should feel comfortable, like a familiar piece of clothing — not foreign or lofty or the way you "should be." And it shouldn't be too long. Keeping it to six values maximum is a good idea. Most of all, engage this process with a spirit of playfulness; be willing to deviate and make up new rules. Even if everyone agreed on just one value or quality — that would be a huge success!

 Imagine a New Way of Being

A JOURNALING EXERCISE

Close your eyes for a minute and place one hand over the center of your chest. Take a deep breath. Observe with curiosity and compassion whatever thoughts and feelings this chapter has stirred up for you. When you're ready, explore the following:

- How would it look if everyone in your family agreed on the same nonnegotiables?
- How would it feel for your family to have a defined and stated culture — would it help guide key family decisions, such as vacations, homework projects, and extracurricular activities?
- How might your relationships or your communication change if your family members were clear on your collective values?

Part IV

EXPLORE A NEW WAY OF BEING

PAUSE for PEACE
Ten Breaths to a New You

Ever wake up in the middle of the night and feel your thoughts spinning like a hamster on a wheel, or have days when you're on the brink of overwhelm and the slightest nudge might send you careening over the edge? Master Li, my qi gong teacher, once told me that when you take ten deep, cleansing inhales and exhales, you increase your energy, enhance your mood, and reduce stress. Try it now: Take ten breaths from your belly, in and out through your nose. They can be gentle or strong; listen to your body. Ahhhh, it works. Often worrisome thoughts just melt away and you're left with a whole new level of perspective. Conscious breathwork is one of our most powerful tools for bringing our minds and our bodies back to home base. Yoga is also an excellent way to develop or learn more about various breathing practices.

Chapter 8

DO LESS,
EXPERIENCE MORE

This past summer, our family was invited to visit friends for the weekend at their cabin on the river, an hour's drive from our house. The night before we were going to leave, my husband and I were frantically creating lists of all the things we needed to buy, prepare, and pack — when we suddenly paused and looked at each other. "What do you most need this weekend?" I asked. He replied, "To stay home and do nothing." I agreed.

So we gave ourselves permission to back out of the commitment and just stay home; our friends understood. We stuck by our guns, too, and had one of the laziest — as well as one of the most connected, soulful, and satisfying — weekends we'd ever had as a family. The high point included lounging in the backyard hammock swing while our son played in the sprinkler with friends. When we allow ourselves to enjoy stretches of unscheduled time, we relax into the gifts that come from doing less and experiencing — and feeling — more.

Many of my clients share that the one thing they crave more than anything is expanses of unscheduled time. I, too, desire more of this, as well as the delights that are born from the space of "doing nothing." At a coaching conference, author and life coach Cheryl Richardson once said that a high quality of life has more to do with what you remove from your life than what you add to it. This is counter to everything we're taught in our modern culture. The idea that the quality of our lives, our well-being, our happiness, and our sense of joy and fulfillment are enhanced when we do less — not more — is a radical departure from the American way. Yet, conversely, we are all too familiar with the stress and exhaustion we create for ourselves when we're overscheduled and overbusy because we've said yes one too many times.

Like many, I find it can sometimes be hard to strike the right balance. I love to try new things, visit new places, and enjoy all that life has to offer, and I often believe I have magical powers when it comes to time management. I distinctly remember one Monday as I juggled work deadlines, emails, and conference calls; AC and car repair appointments; a much-anticipated lunch date with an old friend; an after-school volunteer project with my son; and upcoming visits from out-of-town family members — and feeling a tightness developing in my chest and waves of overwhelm lapping at my feet. As I tried to consciously slow down my breathing, I found myself half smiling in recognition of my old familiar habits.

Yes, some things I was doing that Monday required timely or immediate attention, but much of it could have been declined, postponed, rescheduled, or delegated. I could have slipped off my Wonder Woman cape, asked for more help, and surrendered to the realization that I was simply trying to do too much.

One evening, my friend Joyce declined an invitation to meet to brainstorm on her new business. She was a massage therapist and had an appointment that ended at 6:30 P.M.; we were supposed to meet at 7:30. Joyce said, "Renée, I am so looking forward to seeing you, but an hour is simply too little time for me to transition. I'll feel too rushed. Let's reschedule for another day." Who is your role model for how to graciously flow — not fly — through the day?

Sara, a mom of two, is masterful at keeping it simple. She and her family purposely moved into a community where everything they need is within a walk or bike ride of their home. Quite often when I visit with her at the end of the weekend, she sounds relaxed and rested. One day I asked her how her weekend went, and she replied, "We said no to about half the invitations we received for weekend activities and just stayed close to home. Our goal is to enter each week feeling renewed — not depleted."

Monday-morning phone calls with friends often sound the same: they're exhausted from too many weekend activities, errands, and obligations. What they really needed was rest, rejuvenation, and lots of downtime. Hopefully, this chapter will help you be more like Sara and less like me on that stressful, crazy Monday. Because who wants to be stretched too thin trying to do everything when the result is that our energy gets zapped and we become grumpy, resentful, and often angry — not to mention ineffective?

> *"We're craving more time to just be — so we can actually integrate into our hearts and souls what's happening moment to moment. Overdoing keeps us from having this experience."*
> — Renée Trudeau

THE PRICE of DOING TOO MUCH

We're entering a time of the unknown — a whole new frontier — that I believe requires us to have more space to breathe, think, dream, and digest. We're craving more time to just be — so we can actually integrate into our hearts and souls what's happening moment to moment. Overdoing keeps us from having this experience.

In some real ways, our modern world has expanded what we can accomplish. Things move faster than ever before, we have more options available at our fingertips, and our reach extends around the globe. Yet on a day-to-day level, this comes at a cost to our well-being. Often, we pay the following price:

- We are more distracted. Even when we're together as a family, we aren't present and focused on each other, and we don't feel fed by our time together.

- We are overly focused on activities, goals, and outcomes, which sends the powerful, subconscious message to our kids — and ourselves — that we are only worthy if we're "doing."
- Since we live in constant motion and rarely rest, we are perpetually overextended, and so we become resentful and even angry, at both ourselves and others.
- Physically, we feel chronically tired and exhausted. Our poor bodies, overworked and overstimulated, rarely have time to truly rejuvenate.
- Over time, the ongoing stress from our relentless pace affects our body's immune, endocrine, and hormone systems, which are frequently out of balance. Indeed, long-term stress is the root cause of most disease.

Many of my colleagues in the healthcare and wellness fields — from ob-gyns, therapists, and nutritionists to parent coaches and yoga teachers — have shared how concerned they are with the levels of stress and anxiety they are seeing. They see the effects directly in our bodies, minds, spirits, and children. They are witnessing increasing rates of diabetes, heart disease, strokes, depression, suicide, and other stress-related illnesses. Even my personal ob-gyn said the number one challenge her clients bring up is how to manage stress. The same is true among my own clients and friends: we are doing too much, and crave a slower pace, but we constantly get sucked into the typical "do, do, do — go, go, go" American lifestyle.

That's because many of us have been led to believe that multitasking and being plugged in 24/7 are the only way to stay productive and deliver quality results in our twenty-first-century world. And we're resistant to rest. One of my mentors, Claudia Welch, author of *Balance Your Hormones, Balance Your Life*, says, "If we feel tired, we think something is

> "We make a conscious choice to pause before we say yes to more activity. We keep extracurriculars to a minimum so we can create more breathing room. This has become essential to our family's sanity."
> — Liz, 48, single mother of three

wrong. Nothing is wrong. We are just tired. We need rest. Sometimes a lot of it, if we've gone for years vetoing our body's signals."

We have forgotten how to listen to our body's natural rhythms. We have forgotten what it is like to move through the world at a natural — that is, a normal — pace. When we remember, when we briefly experience it again, it's like a revelation. I remember one summer my family visited the mystical and enchanting Olympic Peninsula on the Pacific Coast in Washington. We hiked through the Hoh Rainforest, soaked in natural springs, roamed lavender farms, and gorged on wild raspberries. We stayed in a log cabin on forty mountainous acres, and at night, we immersed ourselves in stillness and lay on our backs stargazing into a black, oh-so-quiet night. When, my husband and I wondered, did this experience of just "being" become such a rarity?

BALANCING BEING vs. DOING

In our world, balancing being and doing is a constant struggle. We have developed many ingrained ways of being, and changing these bad habits as we embrace new ways of thinking takes time. Proceed with compassion and move gently and slowly.

I've learned to ask myself a series of questions when I'm seeking to come into balance with being and doing. These are:

- What day-to-day choices can I make to feel more grounded, relaxed, and focused? What can I do to live as intentionally as possible each day?
- At the start of each day, what can I do to feel more centered — such as pausing for prayer or meditation?
- What self-care activities will help keep me calm and add spaciousness throughout my day?
- What can I say no to — in both my professional and personal life?
- How can I support my husband and son in being less busy?
- Am I getting sucked into someone else's "busy-ness" and urgency, or am I staying true to what's important to me?

- What choices must I make in order to create more expanses of unscheduled time in my life?

Adopting a new way of being takes time. Keep an open mind and sense of curiosity as you explore what this balance would feel like for you.

When it comes to this topic, I think there are three kinds of people in the world: those whose self-worth rests entirely on "doing"; those who can't relax and play until they've "done their work" (the good old Puritan work ethic); and those who can relax and play at any time and never feel guilty! My husband fits the last category — in his book, "Any time is the right time for relaxing!" — while for most of my life, I have fit the first two categories. I'm very skilled at the "doing dance," and up until about age thirty-five, I preferred to always be in motion. It's alluring and affirming; after all, we are rewarded for output. Do you ever hear anyone say, "Can you believe how often she says no and takes time to just be? Wow, what a role model!"

I desire to experience more equilibrium, and I've made huge shifts in the past ten years; I'm much better about catching myself when the urge to "do" takes over. For instance, one Saturday recently, I found myself in my house alone. For forty-five minutes, I wandered from room to room, not doing much of anything. Then I looked up at the clock and experienced a wave of self-criticism. There was so much stuff I had wanted to accomplish — and I was wasting this rare opportunity of being alone! I felt the sands of time sift through my fingertips as I raced through my mental to-do list — gardening, baking, and cleaning out my closet — and would I really let this gorgeous, sunny day pass without biking?

As each activity flashed in my brain like an overexcited contestant on *The Price Is Right*, I recognized that familiar sense of distraction and irritation. Instead of moving into action, I paused and let it subside. I realized what I really needed to do was nothing at all. So I grabbed an old picnic blanket, headed into our backyard, found the warmest, sunniest spot, and lay down on the cool, welcoming earth — slowly feeling a sense of peace return.

In her book *Inner Peace for Busy People*, mind-body expert Joan Borysenko says, "Remember — your to-do list is immortal. It will live on long after you're dead." To-do lists are seductive. It's as if they shout: "Look how much I'm getting done! See how much I can juggle!" When I was in college,

I took pride in being supernanny for one family I worked for — I made healthy, delicious dinners; I took my three charges on cultural outings and taught them Spanish: and I kept the house picked up, gave them baths, and had them in bed at 8 P.M. on the nose! It hardly ever occurred to me to slow down or pause between errands to see if one of the kids needed a hug after a hard day at school. I rarely sat on the floor with them playing imaginary games with their dolls. I was too busy trying to earn an Olympic medal for how much I could get done. One of my favorite yoga teachers often asks us in class, "Are we here to be productive or to give and receive love?" To me, the answer is clear.

THE SEDUCTION of PRODUCTIVITY

Let's take a deeper look at the busy-bee syndrome. What's really going on here? We know that we are more than our last coup, win, sale, creative project, or completed to-do list, but can we accept that we are enough just as we are?

We've been lured hook, line, and sinker by the seduction of productivity. Our culture is biased to "just do it!" and to "be all you can be," and the perceived reward is our self-worth and self-esteem. This mindset is a root cause of our tendency to overdo and overcommit. Around the water cooler in the office on Monday morning, who gets the most attention and accolades? Is it the guy whose weekend was spent reading and eating watermelon, or is it the woman who went skydiving *and* threw a Brazilian-themed dinner party for twelve?

To counter this attitude, my husband and I gathered a small group of friends for a "Freedom Fest" on a recent July 4. No fireworks, hot dogs, or Tchaikovsky. Instead, we had a potluck and asked each guest to bring one thing that "I want to be free from," such as a habit, worry, situation, or concern.

For me, the first thing that came to mind was email. But as I peeled away the layers of the onion and went deeper, I realized that my frustrations with email were just a symptom of my overall busy-ness. And beneath this was my need to produce and create.

Further, I had good reasons for most of the stuff I wanted to accomplish. I think this is where many of us get caught up in this drive and how it becomes an ingrained behavior. We have positive, even noble, reasons for our busy-ness: it's in service to a good cause, or it's for our family, or to help our community, or to connect with friends, or in the name of healing and world peace, and so on. Pretty soon we've slipped into overdrive, but the only place we're driving to is over the edge. It's just too much.

Throughout the evening, we passed around a basket of freedom questions: What would happen if I was free from _____? When was a time I felt most free? What does being free mean to me? What would feeling free at work, at home, or in my marriage look like? People shared some fascinating perspectives on the theme of breaking free.

Before we all said goodnight, we wrote down all the things we wanted to be free from and burned these outside in a clay pot as a symbolic release.

Days later, as I continued reflecting on the freedom theme, I realized that what we all want most is *inner freedom*. Freedom from our stressful thinking, from our own recurring negative thoughts. We want more interior space. We're tired of living in the shanty built by our own fears and insecurities. We want to live in a mansion — an expansive, wide-open space where we roam free, content, at peace. Where we can breathe deep, long, spacious breaths.

Interior freedom. The space to just be without having to do. Yes, I want to experience more of that for sure. Realize that you can enter that mansion whenever you want, when you disentangle from the idea that your worth is tied to your ability to produce. As my wise mentor Carol Orsborn shares in her book *Inner Excellence: Spiritual Principles to Life-Driven Business*: "Your ordinary self is enough." I'm enough! Without doing. Just me, as I am. What a revelation!

SLOW DOWN...on the INSIDE

Think slow is for slackers? I used to think so, too.

Slowing down and doing less are easier said than done, and they require a radical paradigm shift for most of us. To start, we have to distinguish our inner life from our outward productivity in order to create a lifestyle that sustains us rather than wears us out.

When I was thirty years old, I was a public relations director in a very stressful job. I fit the persona of an overachiever, and I loved the strokes that came with overachieving; I was addicted to having a superbusy mind, schedule, and life. I was also exhausted and frankly doubted I could sustain this pace (really, this level of mental activity — or insanity). Over time, my job, relationships, and well-being were all suffering from my speeded-up life.

So I began working with a great therapist named Frances — she was really a presence coach. Frances teaches clients how to slow down on the inside so that you can actually be more effective and wise in all areas of your life. For the longest time, I thought, "This will never work for me. She just doesn't understand my world. How can I slow down and still get things done?" Successfully juggling and anticipating solutions for ten different projects simultaneously was my hallmark! Slowly I integrated her coaching into my life, and I began to understand the connection between my inner state of being and how I see and respond to my outer world. As I cultivated more awareness for my inner world, it had a huge impact: I lived more in the present, slowed down my thinking, decreased anxiety, and improved my mood in large part by creating more space between my thoughts and my reactions. From stillness also came discernment: I began to see what really mattered to me, and my life purpose and path became clear.

"Reading is a big part of our lives; we like to take time to choose and share books with our children that represent our values and outlook."
— Aidan, 37, father of two

My work with Frances during those years led directly to my work today. It informed the model for balanced living that I teach and try to live by. I have distilled this work into five balanced-living insights: practice "good is good enough," learn to manage your energy, ask for help, practice self-care, and become comfortable saying no. Integrating these five practices or skills into your life can have a profound impact, and they have helped my clients to reclaim their lives, so they are in the driver's seat.

Strategies and Insights for Balanced Living

1. PRACTICE "GOOD IS GOOD ENOUGH." Let go of expectations and the need to please — whether that's about housework, social events, exercise, volunteering, work, or kids' activities. This practice isn't about being lazy or lowering your standards; it's about accepting your best effort for a given task as good enough, so you can devote your time and energy to what matters most, in the moment and at your current life stage. Preparing for your son's fourth birthday party? Invite everyone who matters in his world and serve popcorn and popsicles in the park.

2. LEARN TO MANAGE YOUR ENERGY. When you evaluate the tasks or activities before you, see them in terms of energy, not time. These are not the same, and learning to manage our energy is more important. Some people, situations, and things take more mental and emotional energy than others — such as lunch with a friend who just lost her mom — and we need to allow for this. We can first ask: What today (or in my life) is most important to me? What drains me? What fuels me? What do I need to release? This helps us set our priorities and direct our energy more purposefully and effectively.

3. ASK FOR HELP. This is a biggie, and it can be life changing for those of us who are predisposed to go it alone. But we're all interconnected, and miracles can happen when we allow support into our lives and learn to delegate. Asking for support might mean tapping a potential mentor for advice or asking your kids to help prepare dinner. Sometimes it's help for an actual task, and at other times it may be emotional support as you weather a crisis or challenge. Asking for support can make all the difference in how you experience your journey.

4. PRACTICE SELF-CARE. Don't forget to add your own needs to your daily and weekly to-do lists. Ask: What do I need right now to support my physical, emotional, mental, and spiritual well-being? Then, *tune in*, *listen*, and *respond*. Often, the kindest form of self-care is not overcommitting and overscheduling. Release self-criticism or judgment that you aren't doing enough, whether that's keeping the

house clean or starting a new project at work; this is an essential way to nurture and be more kind to ourselves.

5. BECOME COMFORTABLE SAYING NO. Are you comfortable saying no and not overcommitting? Saying no — to volunteer requests, extracurricular activities, an extra work project, unnecessary travel or trips — is one way we set limits and maintain boundaries. We will need to say no many times in our lives. However, most people find that the more they say no to things that are draining them or pulling them into overwork or overwhelm, the more space they have to say yes to those things that really matter — like reconnecting with your partner or dedicating time to getting your financial house in order. Also, saying no gracefully is a learned skill and it takes practice; there are many ways to do so. For instance, simple is often best; don't trot out a list of excuses. Either decline directly and politely ("No, thanks, I'll have to pass on that") or keep the reason simple ("My time is already committed"). You can also say yes in a limited way ("I can't do that, but I could do this...") or even ask for more time to decide ("Can I get back to you?"). If you're worried the other person will take the answer no as a personal rejection, clarify what you're declining ("I'd love to see you, but this day won't work for me"). For more on this, see the "Nine Creative Ways to Say No" list in my book *The Mother's Guide to Self-Renewal*.

Energy Assessment Exercise

I encourage you to start this process by taking a look at what in your life — outside of work and school — is draining you and feeding you. Set aside thirty minutes this weekend to sit down — either on your own or with everyone who shares your household — and examine what activities in your life energize you and which ones are zapping your life force. Turn off all distractions — TV, radio, phones, and so on — and serve refreshments if you like.

First, each person writes down a list of the activities they have committed to for the next ninety days outside of work and school. If it helps, pull out your calendars to see what you have lined up for the next three months. Most of all, make sure to include all of your social and extracurricular activities:

piano lessons, book groups, dog obedience school, volunteer and committee work, personal travel, vacations, social gatherings, caring for an elderly relative, soccer practice, and so on.

Then, each person evaluates each activity for whether it drains them (depletes their energy reserves) or fuels them (rejuvenates and energizes them). Be honest and be specific. Some activities might be a blend; distinguish as much as possible what refuels you and what drains you about each commitment. How do you know if something drains you? Pay attention to your body. Often when we've landed on a "drain," we'll feel a sense of anxiety or dis-ease in our bellies, upper backs, or chests. (The body always knows!)

Share and evaluate your findings. What are your observations? Do certain patterns emerge? In a family, do some activities fuel some and drain others? Is your list of things that fuel you as long as your list of things that drain you? Are your favorite self-renewal activities on the list of things that feed you?

Finally, call on all your courage and review the list of things that drain you: What are you ready to say no to? What needs to go? Maybe it's all of them! If this seems too radical, think creatively about how you could make incremental changes. Instead of quitting your neighborhood association or your role as Girl Scout troop leader, cut back on the amount of time you spend. Set a "done date," enlist more help, or get support from a mentor or friend about how best to handle the situation. You always have permission to change your mind — your sanity, and your life, may just depend on it.

"Our schedules are busy, so I really feel like I'm doing something special for us when I invest the time to make a meal and enjoy a nice sit-down dinner. We try to do this at least three times a week."
— Deb, 47, mother of two

Support each other in reclaiming your energy and time to do what you really want: for some, that may be nothing at all!

I challenge you to slow down by carefully choosing your activities and where you spend your precious energy; build in downtime and rest. I believe that once you taste the magic of doing less to experience (and feel) more, you'll be hooked!

BALANCING OUR ENERGY: THE DANCE of YIN and YANG

Throughout my twenties and into my early thirties, I pushed myself hard. During my thirteen-year stint in communications, a typical day might involve securing media coverage for a client on the *Today* show, pitching their story to *National Geographic*, then lining up a meeting for them with the French embassy. In between phone calls and meetings, I barely stopped to breathe. I was convinced if I just forced the outcome, I was bound to generate results.

Sometimes this worked; often it didn't. Invariably, this overaggressive mode of operating left me feeling frustrated, overworked, and depleted (not to mention hugely deficient in the fun and joy department!). But also, over time — and as a result of a lot of personal growth work — I came to realize that not all energy is the same energy. I was out of balance, clearly, but in part this was because my energy and how I went about accomplishing things were too heavily weighted in the masculine. I had not yet learned how to tap into my feminine strengths, such as the abilities to ask for and receive help and to pause and reflect before taking action.

Eastern cultures propose that all people, whether male or female, possess both feminine (yin) and masculine (yang) energies, and that individuals are most successful when they honor and utilize both within themselves. Our Western culture — which values results and outcome — is often out of balance because, typically, we overly rely on our masculine, or yang, strengths. However, for some, the opposite is true.

One danger of this yang imbalance is physical and emotional exhaustion and burnout; envision pushing a wheelbarrow full of rocks up a mountain and the long-term effect this will have on your body. More importantly, you are less effective.

Both masculine and feminine energies are important, and our highly intuitive, yin-oriented talents and gifts are necessary. I could not have birthed my first book without tapping my yin strengths — accessing my intuition and waiting until I was ready to begin writing — and my yang strengths — calling on the fire in my belly to execute the timeline and meet the publisher's deadlines! Our real power comes when we learn how — and when — to call both energies forth.

First, reflect on the list below, which outlines a few central attributes of yin and yang energies.

Yin (or Feminine) Energy	Yang (or Masculine) Energy
Intuitive	Directive
Receptive	Goal oriented
Process oriented	Assertive
Collaborative	Authoritative
Flowing	Outcome driven
Relational	Determined
Soft	Hard
Being	Doing

Observe how your body feels as you read each list. Where do you tend to hang out most of the time? Make a list of some of your yin and yang strengths that have supported your personal and professional success thus far. Are you out of balance, one way or the other? Write down a few specific ways you could allow more of your yin and yang qualities to surface. Often, if we find ourselves constantly pushing to make things happen, it would serve us to explore what it would look like to tap our yin strengths — such as listening to our intuition. If you find yourself struggling with boundaries, personally or professionally, ask yourself what would it take for you to own more of your yang strengths — such as being firm and assertive.

Ideally, over time, you will cultivate an awareness for which energy will best serve a given situation. Looking back at many business meetings in my thirties, I can see when, at times, my assertive, directive, focused style kept me from being open, receptive, and collaborative and from listening to what my client really needed.

Envision effortlessly weaving your yin and yang attributes — as you feel guided in each moment — to create a beautiful, strong, sturdy, supple, and flexible straw basket. Some of the ways I balance my yin and yang energies are through dance, yoga, qi gong, tai chi, creative writing, drawing, taking retreats, and journaling. If someone would have suggested this concept to me when I was in the middle of leading a press conference fourteen years ago, I probably would have thought they were crazy. But I've noticed as I've shared the yin-yang principle at retreats over the years, something within this teaching hits many of us — both men and women — at a very deep level.

A NEW SIMPLICITY

Many of us feel called to simplify our lives and do less. Not a fluffy, it-would-be-nice-to-have-clean-closets simplicity, but a new way of being. This new simplicity is about purging and streamlining our thinking, our doing, our giving and receiving, and, of course, our stuff.

We crave more time to just be — so we can actually integrate into our hearts and souls what we're experiencing moment to moment. For some, simplifying might be changing a girls' night out to a girls' night in; voicing clear boundaries to friends, coworkers, or clients about your phone availability; consciously building unscheduled weekends and evenings into your family calendar; moving into a smaller or less expensive home; standing up for what your child or family needs in order to not feel rushed; or maybe serving oatmeal and fruit for dinner.

Ultimately, simplicity is one path to enhancing peace, both personally and in the world. What simplicity looks like for each of us will be different, whether that's living a pared-down lifestyle, getting rid of stuff, taking on fewer obligations, or being mindful about who you let into your life and how and where you spend time. It's about doing and having less, so we open ourselves up to experiencing — and feeling — more.

It's also about realizing and accepting that often the simpler we keep things, the happier we are. I once participated in a writing and movement workshop with men and women of all ages. We were asked to write about what we love for twenty minutes and then read our responses out loud.

It was a cool, rainy Sunday afternoon, and we were deeply moved by one another's simple but profound responses. What do people love? Sleep, rain, cuddling with one's child or pet, holding hands, clean hair, getting a foot massage, making popcorn, the smell of wood shavings and fresh-cut grass. Simple, everyday things. Interestingly, going to Europe, eating a ten-course feast, or gorging on weekend activities like you're at an all-you-can-do buffet wasn't on anyone's list!

"We crave more time to just be — so we can actually integrate into our hearts and souls what we're experiencing moment to moment."
— Renée Trudeau

Our level of happiness and contentment takes a nosedive when we have too many choices or when we are faced with too many decisions all at once. We don't need twenty salad dressing options. We need two, if that.

Simplicity helps us create more space in our lives — something we all want more of. As we know, this isn't necessarily easy to manifest. In fact, we sometimes need to call on our inner spiritual warrior to stay the course and resist the urge to have and do more.

As a review, here are some of the practical, everyday ways you can simplify your life, so that by doing less you experience more:

- PLAN AHEAD. Meet with your partner and children and preview the coming week: Is there anything you need to let go of, reschedule, or postpone to create more spaciousness in your week? Can you build more unscheduled time into your family calendar?
- KNOW WHAT YOUR PRIORITIES ARE. Each quarter, schedule a one-day personal planning retreat and clarify your top three priorities for the upcoming ninety days. Then make sure your activities and to-do lists support these priorities. Use them to help you decide when to say no and when to say "not now."

- GIVE YOURSELF PERMISSION TO SAY NO AND TO CHANGE YOUR MIND AT ANY TIME. Change a "yes" to a "no" if you need to, and voice clear boundaries to friends, coworkers, and clients.

- PAUSE BEFORE COMMITTING TO A NEW OBLIGATION OR SOCIAL ENGAGEMENT. Let yourself sit with and consider it for an hour, or a day or two, before signing on. Ask, "What is my motivation for doing this?" And, "Will this activity enhance my life and sense of well-being or detract from it?" Then act accordingly. If your main motivation is a sense of obligation, or a desire to please or go along with someone else, perhaps let this event or commitment go. Be willing to make the hard, sometimes unpopular choices.

- TAME THE EMAIL AND SOCIAL MEDIA DRAGON. Unsubscribe from lists. Be mindful about overusing these tools and getting lured into the "look how productive I am" mindset. Establish boundaries for when and how often you communicate online, and have set times that you completely unplug (such as in the evenings, on weekends, and so on).

- BUILD IN MOMENTS OF STILLNESS THROUGHOUT YOUR DAY. Create a habit of being to balance all your doing.

- LIVE A PARED-DOWN LIFESTYLE. Get rid of stuff. Go ahead and clean out those closets. If you don't love it, let it go.

- ASK, "IS THIS CHOICE OR ACTIVITY IN ALIGNMENT WITH AND SUPPORTIVE OF MY FAMILY VALUES?" If it's not, reconsider. Less is more. Stand up for what you need in each moment.

When anything feels hard or resistant to change, remember to take baby steps. Adopting just one of the ideas above could make a huge impact on how you experience your days.

Each Monday morning, I start the week by attending a wonderfully nourishing hatha yoga class near my home. When I see friends there, they often ask, "So, how was your weekend?" I like to slowly take this in because it challenges me to pause and check in. When you are asked the same question, how do you respond? Are your weekends "go, go, go," slow as molasses, or somewhere in between? It seems there is always the desire for things to be even slower...and for us to do even less.

Pat on the Back

What's Working?

What is one thing you are doing right now — or have done in the past — to simplify your life so you can experience more time, space, peace, and love?

Putting It into Practice

Do Less, Experience More

Tell your family you're going to try an experiment and you need their help. Pick a weekend day to do nothing. Don't schedule anything the entire day or evening (it won't hurt to miss soccer or swim team for one day). Allow the day to unfold organically (ideally, stay unplugged). It's fine to do whatever the family decides to do in the moment — make popcorn or go for a walk — but the point is to experience what it's like to do less and to enjoy the gifts that come from relaxing into unscheduled time. Notice how and when everyone finds themselves moving into "doing, planning, making it happen" mode. Notice how members of your family are spending time when there is nothing scheduled. Were any gifts born from boredom or from time to just daydream? Afterward, consider: Was it hard to say no to invitations or planned activities? How comfortable are you without a full schedule? What do you observe on your designated do-nothing day? Who has the hardest time with this experiment? Based on this exercise, what does an ideal weekend day look like for your family? What did this experiment teach you?

Imagine a New Way of Being

A Journaling Exercise

Close your eyes for a minute and place one hand over the center of your chest. Take a deep breath. Observe with curiosity and compassion whatever thoughts and feelings this chapter has stirred up for you. When you're ready, explore the following:

- What would it look like for your family to do less — what activity are you ready to release?
- How would it feel for your family to actually create expanses of unscheduled time? What decision do you need to address to make this happen?
- How might the quality of your relationships shift or improve if you started doing less?

PAUSE for PEACE
Give Your Heart a Voice

Think of an issue or problem that has been troubling you.
Close your eyes and ruminate about this problem. Really let it
ping-pong around in your head, unleash the mental chatter, analyze pros
and cons, and see if you come to any clarity. Then open your eyes, pause,
take a couple of deep breaths, and close your eyes again. Place your hand
over the center of your chest or sternum (your "heart center") and bring
your problem down to rest in this area of your body. Fully release
your challenge to your heart — ask for guidance. Keep breathing.
Do you feel any different? Do you receive any insights or
direction? This simple exercise is one I use often.
The heart never lies.

Chapter 9

BREAKING FREE:
MAKING HARD CHOICES

It is 1976, *and my dad has left his booming medical practice in San Antonio. We have abandoned our comfortable, sprawling ranch-style home on two acres and have moved into a twelve-hundred-square-foot home with a wood-burning stove on fifty acres set back on a red dirt road in Northern California's Sierra Nevada. When I am older, my parents will tell me they made the move in order to support a simpler life, to be more connected to nature, and to be near an active spiritual community.*

But right now, I am furious. I hate leaving my friends. I hate the idea of moving to a "yoga community." I'm sure I will never see another Hostess Ding Dong again! Also, I'm nervous and anxious because I have no idea what the future holds. But slowly, as the first year unfolds, I become excited about our new adventure. At school I meet kids from all over whose parents are just as weird as — if not weirder than — mine, and I get to enjoy a tremendous amount of freedom. I study pottery and other arts, and I write short stories while roaming the hundred-acre grounds of our school. Every day, my siblings and I ride horses through undiscovered forests and explore crashing rivers and forgotten trails nestled in tall, inviting Ponderosa pine trees. I find, like my dad, I'm a risk taker. Part of me gets why he is doing this. He — in his own way — is trying to create a new way of being for his family.

Years later, as an adult, I will often joke that all I remember doing during our six years in California is riding horses, reading the Bhagavad Gita, writing poetry, and making stained-glass windows. Yet this period of my life — when I am given the time, space, freedom, and encouragement to really explore who I am — will have a profound and lasting impact on who I become.

My family did what many people say they dream of doing: escaping to a quieter rural life — away from electronics, traffic, overwork, and too many choices. It sounds appealing, but the truth is we don't need to go anywhere to experience what we desire. We are given the opportunity *daily* to make choices that support a simpler, more harmonious way of living.

How have you chosen to set up your life? What choices have you made that impact how and where you work, play, live, eat, spend, and move through your day and life? Ultimately, the question for all of us becomes: What does the life we desire look like, and are we willing to make the choices necessary to experience a new way of being — to embrace greater freedom and joy?

There's a difference between not having a choice and having to make a hard choice. Sometimes we forget that we create our vision for how we want to live. We do. Not our parents, not our kids, pets, friends, or community. We do.

TAKING CHARGE

In the midnineties I worked as a media relations representative for a large international biotech corporation. The culture was typical of most large companies at that time: they expected you to work long hours, and they dangled stock options in lieu of time off. Finding a sustainable work/life balance was never discussed. As a result, I rarely exercised, ate lunch at my desk most days, and took vacations only rarely.

After two years without a break, I decided to take a trip to Europe for three weeks. I made plans to meet up with a group of fellow travelers in Amsterdam (we were all with Rick Steves' Europe Through the Back Door groups), and ten days into the trip, we stopped in Munich and visited Dachau, the Nazi concentration camp where more than thirty-two thousand prisoners were killed. The experience was chilling. Images from the barracks and crematoriums will remain etched in my mind forever.

After the walking tour, I left the group with my journal in hand and settled under a large shady tree to write. I decided to reflect on the question "What is one word that encapsulates my experience at the concentration camp?"

Almost immediately, the image of my job back home flashed through my mind. Suddenly, my body was racked with nausea, and I became sick. Reeling from the intense experience, I sat stunned. What in the world did my corporate public relations job in Austin have to do with Dachau, and why was this connection making me ill?

I looked down. Written in my journal across one page in huge block letters was the word *OPPRESSION*.

Obviously, my life did not compare in any real, direct way to that of the prisoners at Dachau, but I still experienced a visceral, emotional connection to the feeling of being trapped in oppressive circumstances. To that moment, I'd accepted my job and the life I was living as inevitable, but clearly an unheard part of me felt like a doomed prisoner. And this part of me was ready to be released.

A week later, while flying home to Austin from Paris, I heard an interview on National Public Radio with Carol Orsborn, author of *Inner Excellence: Spiritual Principles to Life-Driven Business*. The next day I bought her book and stayed up all night reading it. The following morning I went in to work and (to the great surprise of many) quit my lucrative, international public relations job — stock options and all!

Apparently, I needed to travel to the other side of the world and visit a concentration camp to get that I'm in charge of my career and life path — not anyone else. No one was ever going to come to me and say, "You need a break. Step outside for a walk. It's time for you to take lunch." Or, "It's five thirty. Don't you need to leave to make your six o'clock dance class?" I'm the one steering this ship, and by quitting my job I took the first step in reclaiming my life.

Do you ever wonder how all the day-to-day choices you make, big and small, affect your family and how you live? Do you feel like you're in the driver's seat — that you are the one creating and directing your life with purpose and intent? Or do you feel as if someone else is driving and you're in the backseat, hanging on for dear life?! I often hear my coaching clients say they don't have a choice. They've convinced themselves that they can't change a bad situation. What they really mean is they're unwilling or not ready to make a hard choice, whatever that means — downsizing to a more affordable home, leaving a financially cushy but unfulfilling job, ending an unhealthy relationship, moving to another part of the country, taking a much-needed sabbatical, changing their diet, living on a reduced salary, or changing their lifestyle so it includes exercise and meditation, and so on.

It's so easy to slip into a slumber, to give up control, and to think we're at someone else's mercy regarding how we've set up our lives. But we're not. Every day we are making choices — big and small — that affect our day-to-day life on every level. Some choices are easy, and some are hard and uncomfortable. The key is to choose, and to do so deliberately and consciously, in ways that support our larger life goals — for more freedom, balance, simplicity, harmony, health, creative pursuits, and time to be alone and as a family.

Not all our choices will be perfect, nor will circumstances always cooperate. A few nights after my husband was unexpectedly laid off from his job, he and I sat up late talking about the unanticipated challenges that we were now facing. Instead of being depressed, though, we chose to feel gratitude for all the choices we'd already made that supported our values — specifically regarding where and how to live and work — and that would continue to support us despite our circumstances.

- We live in a home that is beautiful but modest and needs only one salary to cover the mortgage instead of two.

- We live five minutes from my office, which improves my commute and my business's productivity.
- We live close to things that are integral to our quality of life: a yoga and dance studio, hiking trails, a park and community playground, a farmer's market, the Texas Hill Country, and several natural foods grocery stores.
- We live five minutes from our son's school, which further limits commute time each day and expands the amount of time we spend together in the morning.
- And in general, we make day-to-day choices that foster our individual and family well-being: spending time together as a family playing and being outdoors, eating good healthy food, and fostering a deep sense of connection — to ourselves, our family members, and our larger community.

Years ago, I couldn't make it to a photography class early to create prints, and my photography teacher challenged me, stating it was my choice to be late or not. Exasperated, I rolled my eyes and shot back: "You just don't understand. I had too much work — conference calls, media tours — I had no choice!" I really thought I didn't. Now I know I do.

MAKING CHOICES

What do you really want — what is your heart's greatest desire? Are you willing to do whatever it takes to make this a reality for you and your family?

For more than a decade, my company's career-coaching team has worked with thousands of men and women through job searches, career changes, and life transitions. All clients share a similar desire — to find work that is meaningful and that integrates who they are with what they do. When we begin working together, we often ask clients, "What is one of your life goals?" Common ones include writing a book, starting a business or a non-profit, working only thirty hours a week, and living in a rural community. Then we ask, "When do you see yourself getting around to pursuing this goal?" A frequent response is "Maybe when I retire." As our partnership progresses, we challenge clients to move into the driver's seat right now. To get clear on the life they desire and to take the leap to experiencing more fulfilling careers or jobs that are aligned with who they are and that support and serve their life goals. Our everyday lives shouldn't be an obstacle to what we truly desire, but the path itself. To change this, we have to recognize the excuses we sometimes cling to that keep us from fully owning our career and life choices up to now. When we do this slowly and with self-compassion, our life transforms.

Over the years, we've seen

- Ed abandon his stable, high-paying "road warrior" job for one that pays less but allows him to spend more time at home with his family.
- Jack leave software development to launch his own catering business so he could have an outlet for his creativity and passion for food.
- Maya choose a low-stress, forty-hour-a-week job that allows her to pour her energy into her real love: music and playing with her band.
- Eric turn down a vice president position with his current company to keep his lower-stress manager position, which allowed him flexibility to be with his family and parents.
- Susan and David renegotiate their roles to better support their current life stage: David, now a stay-at-home dad, is the primary caregiver for their twins, and Susan, who loves her training job, is the primary breadwinner.
- Doug and Elle sell their big, high-mortgage home and rent a small, modest cottage so they can have more financial breathing room and pay off their debt.
- Janet, a single mom, move into a modest apartment complex near friends so she and her sons could be closer to their support network.
- Jennifer and Joann choose a school and jobs that are less than five miles from their home to cut down on commuting, increase family time, and reduce stress.
- Adrienne and Scott design work scenarios — by taking on more freelance consulting clients and raising their rates — that allow

them to save money so they can take a year off to live abroad with their teenage kids.

I've always considered myself a rebel, yet I remember that after I got married at age thirty-four, I felt a strong drive to buy a house, settle down, and begin having children. That's what society expects us to do, right? Volkswagen even convinced me I needed a "safer" car for my newborn when he arrived!

We're more than consumers. Society, media, and corporate advertisers tell us who we should be and what we should want; these messages affect us in many ways, even when we're not aware of them. One constant message is that we need more stuff — that this new gadget or gizmo will somehow magically make us happy and fulfilled. And we're not just consuming things; we're consuming ideas, values, and expectations. We need to stop, pause, and ask the hard questions about who we are and what we really want or else we'll wake up one day hating our lives — these lives we ourselves have created, albeit unconsciously!

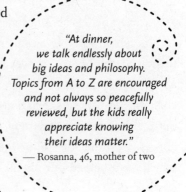

"At dinner, we talk endlessly about big ideas and philosophy. Topics from A to Z are encouraged and not always so peacefully reviewed, but the kids really appreciate knowing their ideas matter."
— Rosanna, 46, mother of two

If we desire to live vibrant, juicy, awakened lives — and I believe we all do — we have to stop sleepwalking. We have to question our assumptions and the assumptions of our culture. Do we believe we deserve to have the life we want? Are we willing to do the necessary inner work to make this happen?

AN INSIDE-OUT APPROACH to MONEY

Just because we set up everything the way we want in our external world — our home, job, and geographic location — that doesn't guarantee happiness. We also have to continue going inward and confirming the alignment of our outer world and our deepest values. Are we returning — often — to our river of inner well-being, which is what sustains and feeds us?

We can't rely on our external circumstances for our well-being, particularly our level of income and bank account. Fears and insecurities around money are often a central issue to tackle before people are willing to make radical shifts in their lifestyle. In order to transform how we work, play, eat, and nurture ourselves, we will inevitably have to face these fears. For instance, Ethan left a lucrative corporate training position to launch a hot sauce business. This was his big dream. He's a cook and an avid foodie, and he comes from a long line of entrepreneurs. Now, like most new entrepreneurs, he is struggling to make his business profitable. To make ends meet, his wife, Jane, works part-time while caring for their two small kids, and the lack of financial stability in their lives is dredging up some of their oldest and scariest beliefs about money.

As uncomfortable as this can be, the most effective response to these fears is to roll up our sleeves and do some financial housekeeping. If fears about money are keeping you paralyzed and unable to pursue major life changes, get your financial house in order — not just by sweeping the porch, but really tackling everything, till you've cleared the cobwebs out of every corner. Consider the following financial health strategies and approaches, which have helped our clients tackle their "inner work" regarding money and prosperity:

- ACKNOWLEDGE YOUR FEARS AND ASSUMPTIONS ABOUT MONEY. When it comes to money issues, we all have work to do. We all have our own "stuff" around money, prosperity, and wealth. What was your family's situation growing up, and is your adult attitude toward money a reaction to it? What are your core issues or insecurities? If money fears are holding you back, are you ready to do the work necessary to release these self-limiting beliefs around the green stuff (which may involve hiring a CPA or a financial consultant)?
- UNDERSTAND MONEY AS ENERGY. Author Joseph Campbell once said, "Money is congealed energy and releasing it releases life's possibilities." In other words, money has no value in itself. Its only value is in what it allows us to do. Rather than accumulating or hoarding money, can you imagine letting it responsibly and joyfully flow in

and out of your life? What if you viewed money as a way to power, fuel, and sustain your life and those areas that matter most to you?

- DESCRIBE YOUR RELATIONSHIP WITH MONEY. If your money was a person, how would you describe the relationship? Is it your best friend, your beloved, or a dreaded enemy you avoid running into at all costs? Does it serve you or are you a slave to it? Is your mood tied to your bank account? Is your self-esteem? Can you imagine living as if your happiness was independent of financial status?

- GET REAL ABOUT YOUR FINANCIAL STATE. Many times we worry about how bad things are without really looking at our financial state. Do you know where you stand financially? Sometimes, we think we're better — or worse — off than we are. However, fear can create paralysis, and the first step to start moving again is to take a full inventory: list your debts and expenses and compare them to you income and assets. Most people have no idea where they stand financially, so just taking this first step is huge. This knowledge can allow you to make conscious choices about how to live and spend.

- EXPAND YOUR NOTION OF PROSPERITY. An antidote to feeling poor is to pause and think of all you have to be grateful for — your health, your freedom, your ability to create, your work, your family and friends, and so on. Money is just one form of prosperity, and sometimes it's the least important. Celebrating all your blessings can help shift your perspective, and it often gives you the breathing room you need to see your situation in a different light.

- SEE THE BIG PICTURE. It's really easy to fixate on our present moment and believe life will remain this way forever. If we feel stuck in our current financial state, remember that this too shall pass. Spend time with friends and colleagues who support you and remind you that your state of being is not determined by your bank account. This is only a bump in the road — you'll survive. We all live in the unknown and no one can predict the future, but we can find our center and choose how to respond to and see our circumstances. As a friend who just lost her house shared with me, "We thought we lost everything, but when we realized we had our health and each other — we realized we were wrong."

• DON'T STOP ENJOYING LIFE! Just because your bank account is lean doesn't mean your life has to grind to a halt. Don't mope — maintain your well-being and keep having fun. Seek out free concerts and events. Go on a family picnic. Go to the dollar theater. Invite friends for a Mediterranean or comfort foods potluck dinner. Enjoy your local and state parks. The best things in life *are* free!

What helps you to feel more empowered about your finances? Many find that when they begin to feel more free, trusting, and open regarding money, they can finally step into the life they truly desire.

DO IT DIFFERENT: EXAMINING YOUR LIFE

Author Robert Puller once said, "Good habits, once established, are just as hard to break as are bad habits."

In essence, habits are nothing more than a choice we make over and over again until the new behavior becomes automatic. If we need to make different choices to ultimately create the life we desire, it may be hard at first, but it gets infinitely easier over time. If you feel called to do things differently, heed this urge and explore what this might look like for you and your family. Question — and be willing to challenge — the choices you've made, and the unhealthy habits you've developed, and see where you can make new ones. Among my clients today, Kurt and Raina are interested in exploring communal living and what this might look like; Maddy and Joe are choosing to rent rather than buy a home, so they'll have more financial flexibility; and many families are exploring how they can live in intentional communities centered around shared values — like green living, education, and sustainable farming.

"What does the life we desire look like, and are we willing to make the choices necessary to experience a new way of being — to embrace greater freedom and joy?"
— Renée Trudeau

Consider the six areas of work, home, play, finances, movement, and food, and examine with curiosity and compassion how you've set up your life. In a journal or with a partner, answer the following questions:

HOW AND WHERE WE WORK:

How do I feel about my work — is it supporting my larger life goals? Is it fulfilling? Is it a fit for my current life stage?

How would I like my work to change — what is missing, and what would my ideal work scenario look like?

How does my partner feel about his or her work?

What action am I being called to explore around this theme?

HOW AND WHERE WE LIVE:

How do I feel about my current home — do I love it? Is it comfortable for my current situation, affordable, and easy to care for?

How do I feel about the location where I live — within my town and within the country?

How would I like my living conditions to change?

What action am I being called to explore around this theme?

HOW WE PLAY:

How do I feel about my lifestyle? Do I have the time I want for play, relaxation, and vacations?

Am I allowing myself to have fun and enjoy the free time I already have?

How would I like my lifestyle/work balance to change?

What action am I being called to explore around this theme?

HOW WE SPEND:

How do I feel about my and my family's spending habits and how we manage money?

How would I like our spending habits to change?

Do I have a clear picture of my family's overall income, expenses, and debt? Do I review this regularly?

What action am I being called to explore around this theme?

How We Move Our Bodies:

How do I feel about my level and type of physical activity? Does everyone in my family get adequate exercise?

What physical activities do I engage in just for pleasure and fun?

Do I spend time outdoors, alone or with others, walking, hiking, and connecting with nature? Are there activities I'd like to do but currently don't?

How would I like my level of physical activity to change?

What action am I being called to explore around this theme?

How We Nourish Our Bodies:

How do I feel about my and my family's diet and the foods we eat? Do we eat foods that nourish us and that are nutrient dense?

What is my family's relationship to food and how we approach mealtimes?

How would I like our diet and food habits to change?

What action am I being called to explore around this theme?

BREAKING FREE and FOOD

Food — how we eat, what we eat, where we eat — is a big deal in America. I've led women's self-care groups for years, and invariably the conversation always comes back to food, meals, and the family diet. This is no accident. A conscious diet is one of the most important ways we nourish ourselves and come into balance — emotionally, physically, and spiritually.

My girlfriend Donna and her family used to consume a Standard American Diet — high in fat, sugar, processed foods, and red meat, and low in fiber-rich, plant-based foods. Recently, however, they've been focusing on eating more healthfully, and they have

"We love to take in new experiences — ones that are new for all of us, like trying Vietnamese food or stand-up paddle boarding. Discovering things together while watching each of us have our own insights is always a good way to learn and grow as a family."
— Steve, 50, father of three

been experimenting with raw foods. Donna doesn't advocate a raw-food diet for everyone, and she isn't sure if this is her path, but she has been so inspired by how much fun her five- and seven-year-old kids are having creating beautiful, bright zucchini-and-spinach "lasagnas," orange-beet soups, and date-coconut balls. She's amazed at how energetic and happy everyone has been feeling and how much pleasure they've received from preparing food together.

Food is medicine. Natural, nutrient-rich foods have the power to heal, nurture, enliven, and foster connection — to ourselves, others, and the earth. They have a huge impact on our mood, energy levels, and daily interactions. I witnessed this growing up in my family: I have brothers who suffer from food intolerances, and my mother spent a huge amount of time and energy creating and nourishing her family through healing foods. She even used her own grain mill to grind flour for homemade millet bread!

I often ask, "What would my body *love* to eat today? What can I choose to eat to express more love toward myself and my body?" Before you say, "chocolate" — pause. I love chocolate, too (as well as cheesy lasagna and chicken pot pie), but this question asks you to dig a little deeper. What would truly nourish you? I've noticed the kinder and more accepting I am of myself, the more nutrient-rich my diet becomes.

I realize that food can be an emotionally charged topic. People often feel strongly about their family traditions, their favorite foods, or their dietary preferences. My family's relationship to food and meals has shifted radically over the past ten years, but it's been a very worthwhile journey with lots of ups and downs and twists and turns. For years, I heard nutritionists talk about the benefits of eating more healthfully, but it wasn't until I had a son and hit midlife that I "woke up" about food. I wanted to feel good and be energized (all the time!), as well as nurture our child.

I encourage you to take this opportunity to explore your relationship to food and your family's diet, and to do so with the utmost compassion, gentleness, and humor. For many of us, food is our primary source of pleasure and even companionship, too. Today, one of my brothers is a macrobiotic chef, but we still laugh about our clandestine, barefoot trips at ages ten and eleven to the neighborhood 7-11 for M&Ms and Butterfingers — only to return home to lentils and brown rice for dinner!

To get you started, here is a list of good questions, strategies, and tips to consider that have helped me as I've shifted my and my family's relationship with food:

- START OBSERVING THE RELATIONSHIP BETWEEN FOOD AND MOOD. How do you feel after you eat? What foods give you energy, sustain you, and make you feel great? Other foods set us off physically and emotionally, and paying careful attention to these reactions led me to eliminate wheat and dairy and limit sugar (three of the biggest food culprits/allergens) in my diet. Today, when I want to feel phenomenal, grilled fish, brown rice, and roasted veggies are the jackpot!

- PAY ATTENTION TO YOUR DIGESTION AND ELIMINATION. What are these telling you about your diet? How do you feel in the hours right after you eat? Not only our emotions but our physical bodies tell us when we're eating right and when we aren't.

- EAT MORE FRUITS AND VEGGIES, REALLY! What helped me shift was the idea of eating a diet that's primarily fruits and veggies and having the other stuff (carbohydrates and proteins) as condiments on the side. Aha! Too bad I didn't listen to my mother's advice when I was in college to always eat lots of "prana-filled foods" — by which she meant fresh fruits and vegetables alive and rich with life force!

- TAKE TIME TO ENJOY YOUR FOOD THROUGH SLOW, MINDFUL EATING. Chew slowly, and in general make eating and mealtimes a pleasurable feast for the senses: play classical music, light a candle, use cloth napkins, set out a vase of wildflowers or herbs, or if it's nice, eat outside!

- ENJOY AND HONOR MEALTIME AS A FAMILY. Make this a time for sacred connection and emotional nourishment, not just a chance to fill your belly. If you don't do it already, introduce some kind of blessing, and make sure everyone has a chance to share about their days.

- GET ADVICE AND FIND YOUR FOOD TRIBE. Are there any authors, teachers, or food gurus who really speak to you? Locate interesting food blogs, recipe sites, and online communities that support healthful eating or a whole-foods-based diet that appeals to you. Find those who share your "food path" so you can support one another in making healthier changes. For some of my favorite natural foods resources, recipes, and recommended books, visit ReneeTrudeau .com/NurturingtheSoul.

- CONNECT TO THE ROOTS! Literally. As much as you can, buy organic, locally grown products; patronize area farmer's markets. If you have them in your area, sign up for a community-supported agriculture program (CSA), in which you receive a weekly share of local, organic fruits and veggies from local farms. Then, visit the farms to see how and where your food is being grown.

- IF YOU HAVE KIDS, INVOLVE THEM IN SHOPPING AND COOKING. Make food a family affair! Encourage your kids to choose veggies and fruits that look and taste good to them, or to choose something they've never tried before; this is a great way to help them learn to attune to their body's needs. Then, as much as you can, involve children in food and meal preparation as well; even if cooking takes a little longer, it's worth it.

- EAT OUT LESS. I love it when my son says, "This stuff isn't as good as what we can make at home!" Instead, replace restaurant outings with fun, healthy food traditions your family enjoys — a Sunday-night fruit smoothie and popcorn party or a Friday-night build-your-own-pizza extravaganza.

- DO WHAT WORKS FOR YOU, START SMALL, AND DON'T OVERWHELM YOURSELF. Little changes can add up to big changes, and these are easier to sustain as healthy habits than trying to change too much too quickly. For instance, instead of ordering pepperoni pizza, order a chicken veggie stir-fry. Instead of cooking one night, make a dinner of healthy prepared foods from a local natural foods grocer or co-op. Think beyond the meal: set out plates of colorful cut-up fruits and veggies for between-meal grazing, and simplify cooking.

Recently, after facilitating an intense women's retreat, I found myself moving down the buffet line at the retreat center dining room. I stopped when I encountered two huge mounds of homemade, fresh-baked currant-and-ginger scones. What a treat, I thought, particularly after all our hard work — but I knew they were made with wheat, which would cause me to feel irritable and tired. So I kept on moving, and I could feel my body smile with delight at being listened to — and loved.

Many times, we already know what we need to do to shift our diet and feel more alive. We just need to listen to that inner voice, follow our gut, and focus on nourishing ourselves, not simply putting food in our bodies. According to the dictionary, *nourish* means "to feed or sustain with substances that promote life and growth."

How are we nourishing and nurturing our family? Are we feeding our bodies and our minds, our hearts and our sense of self, our creativity and our souls? It's interesting to reflect on how our parents "fed" us growing up. My parents chose to forgo expensive vacations and a lot of "stuff" in order to funnel their resources toward Montessori school, music lessons, and an endless stream of books for us. They provided us nourishment through feeding our creativity and our minds, offering us broad exposure to the arts and culture, a diet of natural foods, and many opportunities for self-expression and intellectual stimulation (something I've only recently begun to fully appreciate). I sometimes wonder how my son will describe how we "fed" him years from now. I can only hope he considers it a balanced diet and that we taught him to seek out what he truly needs — with the occasional side of french fries to help keep things in perspective!

AN AWAKENED LIFE

Are you ready to feel more alive? Are you tired of feeling tired? Do you dislike pushing and hurrying yourself and those around you? Are you done with old habits, outdated perspectives, and behaviors that don't serve you any longer? Do you crave space, simplicity, and unscheduled time? Do you desire to live a life that is a reflection of your values and desires?

Breaking free is about being open to the internal shifts and course corrections we need to make if we want to change our outer circumstances.

Now, not next year, is the time to define and claim your ideal life. To embrace and believe in yourself and your worthiness. Not to fix yourself, but to align and expand into the highest expression of who you are. To allow yourself to receive support and guidance for your journey while in the good company of others.

What legacy do we want to leave behind, and who do we want to be in the decades to come? Years ago, my husband, son, and I visited some old family friends — and native Irish speakers — who live in a fishing village outside of Dublin, Ireland. We took lazy cliff walks and farmer's market trips together; we fed the seals in the harbor; we ate fresh mackerel, sea bass, and Irish soda bread with Irish butter every night; and we enjoyed conversations with some of the warmest, most soulful people I have ever encountered. Like many Americans who have traveled in and romanticized Europe, I couldn't stop thinking about how much simpler life seemed there. Yes, sadly, Ireland is becoming "Americanized," but still, the people seem more connected — taking time to enjoy one another in simple day-to-day interactions, treading more lightly on the earth, and eating more whole foods. There seemed to be a strong sense of vitality and vigor in people of all ages, who walked and rode bikes everywhere.

"There's a difference between not having a choice and having to make a hard choice. Sometimes we forget that we create our vision for how we want to live."
— Renée Trudeau

But the thing that stayed with me long after the trip ended was how engaged the elderly were and how they were treated and revered. The Irish seem to give special love and care to the very old and the very young. The older generation was integral to and active in their communities, and they modeled how I'd like to be when I'm eighty: loving, present, and grateful to be alive.

My trip made me realize how quickly time passes — both how swiftly my first forty or so years have flown and how fast the next forty will go. It reminded me that I am making the choices right now for how I want to be and live when I'm eighty. It's up to me.

Living an awakened life calls us to go against the grain — to step off the tracks — and challenge the ideals of our culture to create a life that nourishes us from the inside out, regardless of the opinions of others.

Move slowly; change takes courage and time. As my Irish friends would say in Gaelic: *Tsg go bog I* (pronounced toogguh bug ay), or "Be gentle with yourself."

Pat on the Back
WHAT'S WORKING

What is one way you are breaking free right now — or have done so in the past — and doing it different to support the life you desire?

Putting It into Practice
TAKING A THIRTY-THOUSAND-FOOT SNAPSHOT

The other day I felt completely overwhelmed. Before I let my thoughts spiral out of control, I paused, pulled back, and with my husband's help took a "thirty-thousand-foot snapshot" of my life. Wow, I had a lot going on — more than I realized. I think it's common at times to forget how much we're managing (consciously and subconsciously) — particularly when we're juggling issues that take a lot of emotional energy — and we need to give ourselves a break and take a wide-horizon snapshot that includes all areas of our life. If you took one right now, what would the picture look like? What's demanding the majority of your attention and energy right now? Consider home responsibilities, your children's needs, parenting issues, your career, your day-to-day work, finances, meals and diet, your extended family, your marriage or intimate relationship, your physical health, and even your life stage. If you are in a life or career transition, which can take a lot of extra energy and support, take turns sharing what your thirty-thousand-foot snapshot looks like with your partner or a friend. Enjoy a few deep breaths (and your favorite cold beverage), and give each other a gentle neck or shoulder rub. Perspective is powerful: remember, this too shall pass.

Imagine a New Way of Being

A JOURNALING EXERCISE

Close your eyes and place one hand over the center of your chest. Take a deep breath. Observe with curiosity and compassion whatever thoughts and feelings this chapter has stirred up for you. When you're ready, explore the following:

- What would it look like for you to begin to break free of your old habits — around how you work, play, eat, or move your body?
- How would it feel to make conscious choices (such as how you spend your weekend time) that are in alignment with your greater life vision?
- How might your family life and/or relationships shift if you began to dump old habits and ways that no longer serve you?

Part V

FIND YOUR TRIBE, EMBRACE SUPPORT

PAUSE for PEACE
Allow Yourself to Feel Support

Take a moment to pause, enjoy some deep breaths, close your eyes, and envision yourself completely supported in all areas of your life: on the home front, in the parenting arena, in all your key relationships, at work, around your life purpose. Let your body relax. Place your hands over your heart. You're not alone. You can let go and trust that all is well. You feel validated, heard, supported, and interconnected to a larger community. You move through your day with ease and grace knowing, whenever you need help, you just have to be receptive and it will appear. It's all around you, all the time. Your support team joyfully assists you in all areas of your life. Now open your eyes and enter your day expecting to be fully supported at every turn!

Chapter 10

BUILDING YOUR SUPPORT NETWORK

One Saturday afternoon, my nine-year-old son ran away from home.

He only went two blocks. He was barefoot and was carrying a cigar box filled with a bookstore gift card, fifteen dollars, and a birthday gift certificate from his uncle for bowling. He told me later this was all he needed to support his new life.

He returned after about fifteen minutes (as my poor husband was cruising up and down the streets frantically looking for him!), but the experience — a first — was intense for all of us.

Later that evening, after a heart-to-heart about the experience, a warm bubble bath, bedtime stories, and many cuddles, my son told me that running away from us was the scariest thing he had ever experienced. "Mom, I felt so alone, so scared. It made me think of all the people out there in the world that feel this way every day, that don't have anyone!"

I think we have all experienced times when we have felt the way Jonah felt, alone and scared. When you've been up all night with a sick child, are feeling insecure about your parenting ability, are disconnected from your partner, are having a hard time adjusting to a new boss or a new job, or are feeling overwhelmed and frustrated with all the balls you're juggling, who do you call?

Do you have friends who are always there for you, who will support you when you're down? Other parents who can act as mentors and help you through difficult times? Professional colleagues or peers who can coach you on how to handle a tough career or interpersonal communication challenge? Do you have groups that meet to offer emotional support and connect through meaningful dialogue?

During a workshop I led for entrepreneurs, one woman — a successful consultant — shared through tears that this was her first experience ever to be in the company of other women and to let down her guard and let in support. It was the first time she had allowed others — whom she hadn't paid — to help her. For the first thirty-five years of my life, I was very similar — an über-independent, figure-it-out-yourself kind of girl. Though I've learned to regularly ask for and receive help — truly, from necessity — I clearly remember a time when reaching out to others for support was alien to me. In particular, when I first became a mom, I remember how hard it was for me to make the switch from handling everything by myself to asking for help from my husband, peers, friends, mentors, and family.

I'll never forget the day my husband returned to work after having been home with me for two weeks with our newborn. Sitting in my quiet kitchen, holding my infant, listening to the clock tick, and blanketed in a postpartum haze, I thought, *This is it. I'm all alone — with a baby!* It was a very lonely and scary realization, and I have never felt the absence of a support system more than I did then.

I also discovered I was not alone in this experience. A year or so later, at a birthday party for one of Jonah's friends, the parents were sitting outside in the family's large, shady backyard eating pizza on blankets. Many of us confided how strongly we felt a lack of support in our lives. Some were sad that their parents were deceased, some that their families lived thousands of miles away, and others that their families lived nearby but were not available to them — whether emotionally or for practical help.

All of us were affected by a culture that stresses independence and that regards reaching out and asking for help as a sign of weakness. This begins at a very young age — the first question most people ask about a newborn baby is, "Is he sleeping through the night yet?" — and the message continues bombarding us everywhere we go. Just recently, I noticed a promotional poster at a major fast food chain that compared their "strong burrito" to the desirable traits of a "strong person." At the top of the list was "doesn't need to ask for help."

In many countries around the world, talking about how to build a support network would be a bizarre and unnecessary topic. My friend Ana grew up in Peru, and she recently returned from an extended stay in her native country with her one-year-old child. She loved going home because in Peruvian culture caring for children is a shared responsibility — shared not only within one's extended family but by the entire village as well. In fact, she said, when necessary, it is not uncommon for women even to nurse one another's babies.

Can you imagine this type of sharing in America today? In my family growing up, our modus operandi was independence and self-reliance. Asking for help or support with any task didn't come easily. In part this was because, while I came from a large immediate family, we experienced a distinct absence in our day-to-day lives of our extended family — aunts, uncles, grand-parents, family friends, ministers, close neighbors — a tribe that we could call on when things

> "Ultimately, I believe that what life is all about is releasing, stretching, evolving, and coming into the highest expression of who we are while in community.... Support can make all the difference in how we experience the journey."
> — Renée Trudeau

got stressful. But also, my siblings and I rarely even asked our mom and dad for help. Going it alone was almost a point of family pride or a genetic trait. Both my paternal and maternal grandmothers, who played powerful roles in my life, were strong, entrepreneurial, even eccentric spirits. My mother was also decidedly independent (one of her favorite songs was "I Am a Rock" by Simon and Garfunkel), and I remain amazed at their collective strengths, talents, and accomplishments — single parenting; managing a two-hundred-acre horse ranch; securing graduate degrees; investing, launching, and financing a restaurant while holding down a teaching job; mastering five musical instruments; raising ten children. Ironically, the one thing that I had to teach myself was that I didn't have to go it alone. I could ask for help.

My journey to learning to ask for support has been a slow one. One motivation to make this change came through observing others. I started to notice that people I really admired — those who seemed to experience more balance, integration, and emotional health and resiliency — had strong support systems in place, and they were comfortable stating their needs and asking others for help. Eventually, it occurred to me that this didn't represent a weakness; it's what made them strong! They showed me the gifts of interdependence. It's not just acceptable to need others; it's in our innate nature to give and receive help. We are meant to experience community and connection, to lean on each other, not just when things get tough — but every day!

THE BENEFITS of HAVING a SUPPORT NETWORK

Over the years as a career and executive coach, I have observed that people who are comfortable asking for and receiving help — whether that's from a coach, a therapist, a mentor, a friend, a professional organization, or a business partner or colleague — experience greater success and feel more connected and confident at home and at work. One day at an executive team lunch, I asked the company's CEO if he had ever been scared to initiate risky big business deals — mergers, buy-outs, going public. He said, "Hell yes, I was scared — often terrified! But I had an army of support surrounding me or I wouldn't have been able to pull it off."

Having a support system can have a huge impact on how you experience day-to-day life. Research shows that individuals who have robust support systems

- are more effective in all aspects of their lives;
- keep resolutions, particularly those involving their health and physical well-being;
- weather personal and professional challenges more easily;
- are less likely to feel overwhelmed and find it easier to maintain perspective;

- stay healthier on all levels — mentally, physically, and emotionally;
- are less likely to feel isolated (which can lead to feelings of despair and failure);
- experience less stress and burnout; and
- have children who are comfortable asking for and receiving help from others.

In my own life and work, I've seen the truth of this over and over: feeling supported while moving through a transition or facing a challenging issue can make all the difference in how you experience the journey — and how your family does as well.

Sarah, a mother of two, confided, "When Bryan goes out of town for work for a week or longer, I know solo parenting will be challenging. I have finally learned these are the times I need to heap on the extra support. I usually ask my younger sister to babysit one night during the week so I can enjoy a quiet dinner out with a girlfriend, and I have our high school neighbor come over three nights during the week to help with dinner, baths, and bedtime. I also make sure I have frozen dinners or easy-to-prepare food in the house. I used to dread these business trips. I would want to dump the kids on my husband the minute he returned from his trip and run out the door to get some time for myself. It took a while, but I finally learned that I just have to build in extra support when he's away on a trip. Now, not only are the weeks he's traveling more peaceful and enjoyable, but my husband returns to a family that's happy to see him, rather than resentful that he's been away."

However, our support networks help us even when we don't have a specific need. More than ever before, we're all craving community, and there are many benefits to gathering in small, intentional groups to share and explore what matters most. Humans have a strong desire to come together — not as a leisure-time luxury, but as a necessity. We need each other. And we need "belly time" — not just texts or Facebook updates.

We receive many gifts when we gather intentionally to feed our hearts and souls:

> *"Daily hugs and kisses in the morning, making sure we say 'hi' and 'bye' when we come and go, and telling each other 'I love you' a lot (and meaning it!) helps us feel more connected."*
> — Carissa, 38, mother of three

- When we allow ourselves to become vulnerable and open up to help, we embrace our interdependence and tap into one another's wisdom on the deepest level. We realize we're one another's teachers.

- When going through a challenging time, reaching out to and gathering with like-minded friends for authentic conversation helps us feel validated and supported.

- Being with good friends who care deeply about us reminds us who we *really* are. They help us remember our stuff isn't the "biggest thing that's happening to us," it's just the "biggest thing in this moment!"

- When we ask for help or gather in groups, we experience our interconnectedness directly, so that we don't feel alone.

- When we gather intentionally around a common theme, we realize how much our experience is shared by others. Having our friends or community articulate what we've been feeling in our own hearts can elicit an immediate shift in perspective or an aha moment!

- The practice of being real, vulnerable, and deeply authentic in front of others — as my mentor says, "showing up warts and all" — can be amazingly cathartic and freeing!

- When women gather in groups, our physiology changes: our immune systems and serotonin levels get a boost and we release oxytocin (the cuddle hormone) — which results in us feeling calmer and happier overall.

Finally, the act of giving and receiving support can be a spiritual practice. This is particularly true during times of extreme need — just ask anyone who has faced a major illness or has cared for a child with special needs. Occasionally, life forces us to surrender to divine grace and call in the troops!

LEARNING to ASK for HELP

We all need support — lots of it. We weren't meant to do everything for ourselves. Assess how you currently navigate challenges: Do you immediately isolate, put on your armor, grab your sword, and head out into the forest to slay the dragon alone? Or do you enlist the help and strategic counsel of other knights and soothsayers who have already weathered similar challenges? What is your typical response to feeling stressed, overwhelmed, and isolated?

Next, consider all the ways you could ask for the help you need. What do you do now that you could do more often, or what new steps could you take? Regardless of the challenge — whether it involves parenting, your career, or a relationship issue — consider expanding your concept of what it looks and feels like to receive support.

Here are a few ideas on how to ask for and receive help in our everyday lives:

- Let your boss know you're overextended at work and you're concerned this will effect the quality of your work. Specifically, you can ask for help prioritizing tasks, request additional staff support, or tap coworkers for help or ideas on how to streamline processes or tasks.
- Cultivate an existing friendship, or create a support group that will meet your specific needs.
- Ask a neighbor, another mom or dad, or a single friend to watch your child when you need help. Don't feel like you have to reciprocate; just practice receiving. If a friend or neighbor has offered help in the past, don't be shy about taking them up on it.
- Reach out to a career, leadership, or business coach for support on making a career change or navigating a challenging phase in your professional life.

- If you usually handle the cooking, ask your partner to make a meal for the family — and then stay out of the kitchen. Let go!
- If you have a big house chore to handle, like cleaning out your garage or weeding your yard, create a "work crew" of friends. Reward them with a party afterward, and/or offer to swap house tasks the following weekend.
- For family or parenting issues, ask for support and ideas from a parenting educator or coach. Often churches or local nonprofits offer this for free. If you're unsure, ask potential mentors to lunch to get to know them first.
- If you want more emotional or practical help from your partner, set up a date to talk about this and brainstorm ways you could support each other to bring more flow and ease to your days (sometimes you may simply need emotional support).
- Get your kids involved. Ask them to help fold the laundry, vacuum a room, help with dinner prep, or water the plants. Kids are never too young to share in household or family responsibilities.
- Practice saying yes! The next time someone offers you something — to buy you coffee or lunch, to watch your cat, to help you move, and so on — accept the gift, smile, and say thank you!

In our Personal Renewal Groups for women, we designate one entire month for "Building a Support Network." Because so many of us find it hard to receive without feeling that we have to immediately give in return, the homework challenge is to practice receiving support by "allowing" others to help — picking up the kids, running an errand, mailing a package at the post office, receiving a meal — and not reciprocating. I believe because we're so conditioned to do for others and often put ourselves last, women always find this really difficult. Yet at the same time, they share how deeply rewarding it is to help out and support others just for the joy of it — with no expectation of receiving anything in return. In everyday life, there's nothing wrong with offering to return a favor ("Thanks for watching Scott; I'll be happy to watch Elijah next week"), and most people do this often, but I challenge you to balance this with learning the art of receiving without feeling that you owe the other person a thing.

The more comfortable we become modeling giving and receiving with ease, the more our children will learn to do this, too. It's like building up your support muscle — it takes time and practice.

Maddy, a friend who facilitates our self-renewal circles, once told me she found her four-year-old daughter, Ella, creating a circle on the floor with all of her dolls and animals propped up on pillows. Ella said proudly, "Look, Mama, they're having a Personal Renewal Group meeting to help each other!"

FINDING and BUILDING YOUR TRIBE

I'm passionate about fostering connection and creating intentional community for myself, my family, and others. I'm involved in so many groups that when I'm headed out the door to an evening or weekend gathering, my husband likes to joke, "Which women's circle, girlfriend gathering, or retreat are you going to or leading today?" My husband has learned to find his tribe, too, participating in a weekly drumming group — for over seven years — and attending an annual men's spirituality retreat.

Building your tribe takes work, however. It's a skill that we have to learn. And as I travel around the globe, I frequently hear the question "How *do* you create community?" A female executive at a large Fortune 500 company came up to me at the end of a "build your support network" presentation in Philadelphia. She had tears in her eyes. She said that while she was in a book club, involved in her neighborhood, and occasionally attended women's leadership discussion groups, what she sorely missed and craved most was real, authentic, meaningful dialogue with people who let her show up without her mask — makeup-free.

Finding such a community of people may be just a conversation away, but it requires us to let down our guard, be vulnerable, and open up to a new way of being with others. People everywhere have a growing desire to circle up and connect more deeply around matters of the heart. It's how we're supposed to be, and when you experience this, there's no turning back. Before you can find or build that community for yourself, however, you must cultivate the mindset and desire to make this a priority; you set your intention for how you want to interact with others before you ever take action.

Even during my busiest seasons at work, I'm always looking for meaningful ways to gather women; this is and always will be central to my life. In honor of what would have been my nonnie's (my maternal grandmother) hundredth birthday, I gathered a small group of close friends to honor and celebrate the gifts we have received from our grandmothers — living and deceased. We each brought our grandmother's favorite food, her photograph, and a physical object that represented one of our qualities that we attributed to her. After enjoying a meal together, we circled up and took turns drawing names from a basket and then bestowing these "gifts" upon each other. I received a circular seashell from my friend Amy, which represented her nana's art of bringing people together — it was perfect.

"Susan and I both grew up feeling isolated, so it's important to us that our son knows we're part of a larger community — neighbors, teachers, church group, family campouts — and that we're all here to help each other out."
— Julie, 49, mother of one

Building and facilitating community is core to my being, and it's radically transformed my life. Whether it's reaching out to a mentor for support on a new project at work or emailing my meditation circle to ask them to send me good thoughts when I'm having an emotionally turbulent time, I now know that if I'm feeling alone — it's my choice. And I can choose not to be.

Create a Personal Support System

Envision moving through your day and feeling totally supported in all areas of your life: around self, at work, at home, in your marriage and parenting, and in your volunteer and community activities. You don't have to have all the answers; you're not alone, and you have a robust team you can call on for help in all areas of your life.

Use the following exercise to create your new support network and get specific about what kind of support you need and want in the key areas of your life. Acknowledge those who are currently supporting you and think about your needs and what type of support you need to add.

On an oversize sheet of paper, draw a large circle and put a recent photograph of yourself in the middle. Using colored pens or pencils, divide the circle into four quadrants or categories; as in the table below, I suggest work and community (which can also encompass volunteer work), self, family and marriage (your key relationships), and household (which can include household maintenance, cleaning, cooking, and so on). Then, fill in each section with the names of people or positions (such as "career coach") who could make up your ideal personal support system. Draw lines or "rays of support" radiating out from you toward the outer edge of the circle (like spokes on a wagon wheel) and write each name or position on the lines within the corresponding quadrant. (See the example below.)

Everyone's support system will be unique. Include people you already know as well as people, organizations, and positions you need to find or get to know. Remember, this is about mapping out what you need to feel fully supported where you are right now!

Following is a list of individuals and resources you may consider including in your support network:

- professional and personal mentors
- professional development and networking organizations

- professional or skills-based teachers, instructors, or trainers
- work/life balance, business, or career coach
- professional peers and colleagues
- friends with kids
- friends without kids
- neighbors
- play groups, parenting support groups, and parenting coach
- single-parent or special-needs support groups (such as the Down Syndrome Association)
- babysitting and child care providers, such as daycare, nanny or sitting services, child care co-ops, co-working spaces offering childcare, and pediatricians
- social groups: creative or hobby groups, book clubs, and activities just for women or moms
- therapist, counselor, or support group
- spiritual mentors and communities
- financial consultants or advisers
- online support communities, forums, tele-classes, and so on
- family members
- meal co-ops and meal-delivery programs
- home care or repair, cleaning, and yard care services
- bodywork and health specialists, such as physicians, ob-gyns, chiropractors, acupuncturists, massage therapists, women's health/hormone specialists, nutritionists and health coaches, physical therapists, and so on

As you create your support network, keep a few things in mind. This is meant to capture what you need to feel fully supported for your current life stage, needs, and family situation, but you, your family, and your support system will change. I recommend doing this exercise at the beginning of each quarter or at a minimum twice a year. Further, choose people you trust and admire for their experience and insight to be a part of your support system. Enlist the support of those whose lives reflect your own values and beliefs. Be selective. Don't include people you feel you should simply because they are family or you've known them for a long time. In fact, if relationships are strained, it may even be unhealthy to try to enlist family members as part of your support network.

Don't hold back — think in terms of your ideal. What type of and how much support do you really need to live, work, and parent optimally?

Finally, post this drawing where you will see it — maybe in your kitchen or home office, where it can remind you that help and support are only a phone call or email away. In fact, consider converting your support wheel into a list of phone numbers you can keep in your purse, by your computer, or on a bulletin board. It is often reassuring to have these names and numbers within arm's reach. Share your new support network with your partner or a friend (and encourage them to create their own support wheel). Then, if you've identified support that you would like but don't yet have, turn this into an action list: who can you call, or what groups can you start or create, to provide the support you need? (See "Putting It into Practice" below.)

When my son was small, I had a bulletin board in my kitchen with a picture of my family in the middle and an affirmation in large type at the top that read, "I Manage My Life with Ease and I Experience an Abundance of Time and Support." On the board, I posted lists of various support areas with phone numbers. In part, this was a practical tool: it helped to have handy the contact information for moms and friends, play groups, my health and wellness support, babysitters and child care, therapists, parenting coaches, and so on. But more importantly, I would feel a wave of support wash over me every time I looked at the board and visualized my support system, ready to spring into action when needed. Now, I just have to keep remembering to reach out and ask for help through all my life stages!

FLIPPING on the SUPPORT SWITCH

Learning to ask for and receive help isn't something that happens overnight. For most of us, this takes some inner work, releasing control, lots and lots of practice, and often rewiring some of our habits and expectations.

One afternoon at work, a team member surprised me with the news that she was heading out of town and wouldn't be available to help me prepare for several upcoming national events. I panicked, translating this into the thought, "I'm not supported in the world," and felt a strong tidal wave of emotions sweep through my body.

Then something interesting happened.

Less than an hour later — after ten minutes of slow, deep, conscious breathing while sitting in my car outside my hair salon preparing to go in for a cut — I heard a clear, kind voice say, "You know that's not true. You are abundantly supported." Then a collage of images representing all the ways I was supported in my life flashed before my eyes.

This truth landed internally like a hundred-pound anchor, and as I resonated with these words, I felt something inside me "dislodge." It was as if I was being rewired in that moment — as if my internal blueprint for how I see and respond to life was shifting. I had tapped into the wisdom of my body and my real truth: I was supported in many, many ways.

Ultimately, I believe that what life is all about is releasing, stretching, evolving, and coming into the highest expression of who we are while in community. Who would choose to go it alone when you can walk your path in the good company of your brothers and sisters? Support can make all the difference in how we experience the journey.

Pat on the Back

WHAT'S WORKING?

What is one thing you are doing right now — or have done in the past — to reach out to others and ask for help?

Putting It into Practice

ASKING FOR HELP

Now that you've created your new support network, this is a great time to practice asking for the help you need. Reviewing your support wheel, which quadrant jumps out right away as the area that most calls for your attention? Within that quadrant, if you were to choose one specific need (such as a career coach to help explore a career change or a parenting mentor to help navigate issues with a teen), what would it be? Before you leap into action, schedule some time to briefly explore the theme of asking for and receiving help by responding to the journaling questions below. Doing a bit of inner work before you take your first steps can make the process easier. Have your journal nearby to record additional ideas or thoughts that come up around this theme. Share your answers with a friend or your partner.

- How did my family approach the issue of asking for and receiving help? Who in my family modeled this for me?
- What limiting beliefs or thoughts do I need to release in order to become comfortable asking for help?
- Who in my life is good at utilizing a support system, and what do I admire about them?
- What do I see as the primary benefits of learning to ask for and receive help?

Then, when you're ready, take that first step and go find the support you need. If you're seeking a new resource and feel stumped as to where to begin, asking friends and parenting or school groups is always a great place to start.

Imagine a New Way of Being

A JOURNALING EXERCISE

Close your eyes for a minute and place one hand over the center of your chest. Take a deep breath. Observe with curiosity and compassion whatever thoughts and feelings this chapter has stirred up for you. When you're ready, explore the following:

- What would it look like to take the first steps toward allowing support into my life?
- How would it feel to be more supported — personally and professionally — in all areas of my life?
- How might my family life and relationship shift if I began to ask for and receive more support?

PAUSE for PEACE
Take an Energy Shower

As you step into the shower this morning, take a few
moments to close your eyes and enjoy the warm water cascad-
ing over your shoulders. Then, keeping your eyes closed, begin to
wiggle your toes, bringing all your awareness into your feet. Invite this
energy to move up to your ankles, calves, knees, and thighs — the whole
time staying present to the sensations in your body. Envision this energy
moving up your thighs into your pelvis, your hips, your abdomen and torso
— bathing your organs in light — and feel it travel out through your chest,
across your arms, and over your hands, while simultaneously moving up
your neck, into your head, and pouring out through the crown of your
head. Take a minute to feel how alive and present you feel and what a
wonderful gift it is to be in your beautiful, vibrant body. Feeling this
energized in — and appreciative of — your body is a great way
to begin the day! If you wish, imagine the energy is a
specific color that feels healing to you. You can also
do this sitting or lying down or during a bath.

CONCLUSION

Imagine this:

You walk into your kitchen on a Saturday morning feeling rested, relaxed, and eager to connect with your family. You feel the sun streaming in through the windows, bathing your face. Despite the typical morning noises — maybe even chaos — in your household, a quality of stillness underlies everything. You're looking forward to being with your tribe and seeing what the day may hold for you. Grateful that you have kept weekend activities to a minimum, you and your family sit down at the kitchen table and leisurely enjoy some yogurt and blueberries together. Your heart is open and receptive, you are present, you listen to one another with curiosity and compassion. You acknowledge the gift of one another — of having this time together. You feel contentment, gratitude, and joy pool in the center of your torso and spread out through your limbs. There is no task, place, or obligation that is more important than being right here, in this moment, with each other. You smile with the realization that this is the life you desire — that the feeling of inner peace and trust surging through you right now is who you really are, and it has the capacity to guide all that you do. You've come home.

What can bring you to this place? What insights, perspectives, or tools from *Nurturing the Soul of Your Family* resonate with or speak to you and can support you in feeling more connected to your family? What habits, perspectives, and thoughts can you embrace — or release — in order to step into a new way of being and come into a higher expression of who you are — as an individual and as a family?

I remember taking a family trip to the beach when Jonah was around three. Off and on throughout the weekend, I felt irritated at how hard parenting seemed, frustrated at how disconnected I felt from my partner, overwhelmed by how much work I was juggling, and unable to relax. I experienced fleeting moments of peace — listening to the waves, watching my son and husband feed the seagulls — but most of the time I sat on the beach stewing in my negative habitual thoughts, reading personal-growth books, and, if I was really honest, viewing myself as a self-improvement project that still had a long way to go. The deeper truth — that my true nature was peace and well-being, and I just had to choose to return to this — had flown out the window with my son's red balloon on the drive down.

We need constant reminders that anchor us to the truth of who we really are. Family life is messy, unpredictable, beautiful, and complex. Sometimes it feels like we're showing up at a new job each day with no instruction manual. The highs can be euphoric; they give our lives meaning and remind us why we signed up in the first place. The lows can bring us to our knees and make us want to take the first plane out of here; they teach us more about ourselves than we might want to know — or are ready to hear.

The ten paths to peace in this book are doorways or invitations to help you remember how to reconnect with those you love most so you can find and experience more peace and more harmony — every day. They help you return to your river of well-being — in the middle of homework squabbles, making dinner, work meetings, disagreements with your partner, and daily commutes. You don't need to take a retreat, travel to India, or carve out three hours a day to meditate to find this. I challenge you to give yourself the space and time to fully explore this book. It can change your life if you let it. Allow yourself to be cracked wide open and let the light in — and out.

And I encourage you to engage your kids in this process. What do they most want from you? What do they think enhances your family's sense of peace and harmony? What do they think derails it? Ask them. Have you told them how important your family — your tribe — is to you and how strongly you desire to feel connected to them? When things get rough, do you take time to sit down with them and, if needed, share a heartfelt apology, explain any stress you're feeling, and allow them the space to ask questions or express what they're feeling?

In spring 2011, my family visited Big Bend National Park — one of our favorite spots. It's truly off the grid, so remote you can travel for days across its eight hundred thousand square miles and not see a soul. One afternoon toward the end of our trip, after a long hike through the Santa Elena Canyon, we stopped at a park campground for a snack. As my husband turned off the car, I heard a strong but insistent whisper in my ear, "Grab some paper and a pen." I resisted. "What?! I'm busy. We're about to relax, and my stomach is grumbling." The voice and urge were persistent and strong; without saying a word to my family, I dug in my backpack for my journal and a pen, grabbed a Mexican blanket from the backseat, and plopped down on the grass next to the car under the two-hundred-year-old singing cottonwood trees. What poured from me — really, it came through me — over the course of about fifteen minutes are the ten paths to peace described in this book. I have always been a "writer in service." I don't initiate anything — an article, project, or book — until I'm divinely guided to do so. And this was undoubtedly one of those times.

By reading this book, you show that you take the role of conscious parenting to heart. Staying awake, present, and engaged on this path requires courage and the willingness to continually make big and small course corrections. Yet we all need reminders that help us stay awake on the path. Here are mine:

• Remember that it's no mistake we're together: Conscious parenting is at heart a profound spiritual exploration of the mystery of how and why your family came together.

- Know your ordinary self is enough: Our job is not to fix ourselves or each other but to tap the insights and tools that support us in coming into the highest expression of who we are.
- Continually ask, "What if": Invite in curiosity, playfulness, and wonder as you navigate your relationships and day-to-day experiences and explore what's possible.
- Be open to a new way of being: Be bold. Be willing to step off the beaten path and to take the road less traveled. Practice living inside out, and do it different.
- Be compassionate and loving with yourself: Above all, treat yourself as worthy of the same self-nurturing, acceptance, and tenderness that are afforded to our children.

Singing is one of the quickest and most powerful ways I know to bring a group of souls together and to feel one another's hearts. I learned one of my favorite songs at my son's preschool. It has been around since the 1960s and is sung in many circles — from school groups to yoga classes to community gatherings — around the world. May the beauty of this song and its message surround you and your family in love, remind you of the pure light within you, and guide your way home — to yourselves and to one another.

May the Longtime Sun

May the longtime sun shine upon you
All love surround you
And the pure, pure light within you
Guide your way home, guide your way home

ACKNOWLEDGMENTS

My heart overflows daily with gratitude and joy for all the ongoing support in my life. This project was especially blessed by assistance from the Renée Trudeau & Associates and Career Strategists team — Sara, Sarina, Angie, Bren, Angela, Taylor, Brooke, Dana, Chloe, and MJ; the dedicated *Nurturing the Soul of Your Family* advisory team — Ellen, Liz, Sara, Carissa, Jolie, Melissa, Anne, Rebecca, and Rhonda; my beautiful Moon Sisters Meditation Group — Deb, Dianna, Celeste, and Carolyn; our soulful community at the Primavera Montessori/Khabele School; the amazing tribe of teachers and students at my second home, Yoga Yoga; my Freedom Sisters Mastermind Group — Bella and Susan and the brilliant women in my Enlightened Entrepreneurs Collective; and Deborah Kern's soulful Daring Divas Dance community. I am grateful for the steadfast support of my colleagues and mentors: writing and creativity coach Carolyn Scarborough, presence coach Frances Cox, the wildly generous Jennifer Louden, my dearest Margaret Keys, spiritual teacher Hiro Boga; the well-balanced publishing

counsel I received from my agent, Stephanie Kip Rostan, with Levine Greenberg Literary Agency, and the amazing New World Library publishing team — especially my patient and supportive editor, Georgia Hughes. I extend a huge bear hug to my biggest supporters on earth — my beloved life partner, John, and the light of my life, Jonah; thank you for encouraging me to keep expanding into what I'm here to do. From every aspect of my being, I am deeply grateful to God — the source and energy that so beautifully inspires, guides, and feeds each and every one of my creative projects. I am honored to serve.

NOTES

INTRODUCTION

Page xix *He says when people are asked to envision the future*: Richard Louv, *Last Child in the Woods: Saving Our Children from Nature Deficit Disorder* (Chapel Hill, NC: Algonquin Books, 2005).

Page xix *Author and futurist Barbara Marx Hubbard, in her documentary* Humanity Ascending: Barbara Marx Hubbard, *Humanity Ascending*, 2007, http://www.humanity ascending.com/index.html.

CHAPTER 1: THE TRANSFORMATIVE POWER of SELF-CARE

Page 10 *In* Slowing Down to the Speed of Life, *authors Richard Carlson and Joseph Bailey*: Richard Carlson and Joseph Bailey, *Slowing Down to the Speed of Life: How to Create a More Peaceful, Simpler Life from the Inside Out* (New York: HarperCollins, 1989), 125.

Page 12 *My favorite quote from Goethe is taped to my computer*: Johann Wolfgang von Goethe, quoted in Stephen Covey, *Seven Habits of Highly Effective People* (1989; reprint, New York: Free Press, 2004), 146.

CHAPTER 2: PEACE BEGINS with ME: A JOURNEY to WHOLENESS

Page 27 *Actor Larry Eisenberg reminds us, "For peace of mind"*: Larry Eisenberg, *Bulletin Boarders: Two Thousand Statements for Bulletins, Sign Boards, Posters and Bulletin Boards, Sermon Titles, Wall Hangings* (1973; reprint, Lima, OH: CSS Publishing Company, 2002), 23.

Page 27 *Author and spiritual teacher Byron Katie tells a great story*: Byron Katie and Stephen Mitchell, *Loving What Is* (New York: Three Rivers Press, 2003).

Page 29 *I agree with author Marianne Williamson, who wrote in her book* A Return to Love: Marianne Williamson, *A Return to Love: Reflections on the Principles of* A Course in Miracles (New York: HarperCollins, 1992), 190–91.

Page 37 *Author Richard Carlson says, when you focus on your own healing*: Richard Carlson, *Don't Sweat the Small Stuff—and It's All Small Stuff: Simple Ways to Keep the Little Things from Taking Over Your Life* (New York: Hyperion, 1997), 134.

CHAPTER 3: PEOPLE FIRST, THINGS SECOND: THE DIGITAL DIVIDE

Page 46 *It's worth keeping in mind some of the recent research related to screen time and electronics*: The information in this list comes from the following sources:

The amount of time families spend together each week and *When four- to seven-year-old kids were asked*: USC Annenberg Center for the Digital Future Survey, USC Annenberg Center for the Digital Future, 2010, http://www.digitalcenter.org/pdf/2010_digital_future_final_release.pdf.

Children today spend an average of six hours each day: Statistics from No Child Left Inside, Chesapeake Bay Foundation, http://www.NCLICoalition.org, 2010.

Children and youth from age eight to eighteen: "Generation M2: Media in the Lives of 8- to 18-Year-Olds," The Henry J. Kaiser Family Foundation, January 2010, http://www.kff.org/entmedia/upload/8010.pdf.

Childhood obesity is on the rise: President's Council on Physical Fitness and Sports, "The Role of Family in Promoting Physical Activity," *Research Digest* (March 2010), https://www.presidentschallenge.org/informed/digest/docs/march2010digest.pdf.

On average, each hour of TV watched per day by preschoolers: Dimitri Christakis et al., "Early Television Exposure and Subsequent Attentional Problems in Children," *Pediatrics* 113, no. 4 (April 2004), http://pediatrics.aappublications.org/content/113/4/708.full.pdf+html.

In 2008, people consumed three times as much information and *Our attention is constantly shifting*: Matt Richtel, "Attached to Technology and Paying a Price," *New York Times*, June 6, 2010.

Among Americans, 33 percent say the TV is always on: "How Americans Eat Today," *CBS News*, January 12, 2010, http://www.cbsnews.com/2100-500165_162-6086647.html.

CHAPTER 4: NATURE: THE ULTIMATE ANTIDEPRESSANT

Page 61 *My experiences as a child were not unique, and many scientific studies and books confirm*: Among others, see Richard Louv, *Last Child in the Woods: Saving Our Children from Nature Deficit Disorder* (Chapel Hill, NC: Algonquin Books, 2005), and Cheryl Charles and Alicia Senauer Loge, "Health Benefits to Children from Contact with the Outdoors and Nature," *Children & Nature Network*, 2012, http://www.childrenand nature.org/downloads/C&NNHealthBenefits2012.pdf.

CHAPTER 5: RETURNING to the RIVER: FINDING SPIRITUAL RENEWAL

Page 80 *I took the How to Talk So Kids Will Listen and Listen So Kids Will Talk parenting course*: Adele Faber and Elaine Mazlish, *How to Talk So Kids Will Listen and Listen So Kids Will Talk* (New York: Harper Perennial, 1995).

Page 85 *I once heard Marianne Williamson...say on a radio interview*: Marianne Williamson, Hay House Radio interview, 2011, www.hayhouseradio.com.

Page 89 *Spiritual teacher Byron Katie said at a workshop I attended, "Arguing with reality"*: Byron Katie, workshop at Kripalu Center for Yoga & Health, summer 2007.

Page 93 *At an international coaching conference, I heard author and teacher Tal Ben-Shahar discuss*: Tal Ben-Shahar, seminar, "Positive Psychology: The Science of Happiness," International Coaches Federation, fall 2009.

CHAPTER 6: SPENDING TIME TOGETHER (LIKE YOU MEAN IT!)

Page 110 *For more about this type of sharing, see* Love Tune-Ups: Matthew McKay, Carole Honeychurch, and Angela Watrous, *Love Tune-Ups: 52 Ways to Open Your Heart and Make Sparks Fly* (Oakland, CA: New Harbinger Publications, 2002).

Page 111 *He shares in his book* A New Earth, *"Many children harbor hidden anger"*: Eckhart Tolle, *A New Earth: Awakening to Your Life's Purpose* (2005; reprint, New York: Plume, 2006), 103.

Page 112 "Look at Me": words and music by Sara Hickman, on *Big Kid*, Sara Hickman (Le Petite Bonheur/BMI), www.sarahickman.com. Used with permission.

CHAPTER 7: DEFINING, CELEBRATING, and HONORING YOUR FAMILY CULTURE

Page 120 *Too often, ...author Gordon Neufeld says, "we make children work"*: Gordon Neufeld, *Relationship Matters: Harnessing the Power of Attachment* (The Neufeld Institute, Growth Concerns, and the Arnprior Child & Youth Counseling Centre, 2010), DVD, http://www.neufeldinstitute.com/products/dvds.

CHAPTER 8: DO LESS, EXPERIENCE MORE

Page 138 *One of my mentors, Claudia Welch, author of* Balance Your Hormones, Balance Your Life, *says*: Claudia Welch, *Balance Your Hormones, Balance Your Life* (Cambridge, MA: Da Capo Press, 2011), 222.

Page 140 *In her book* Inner Peace for Busy People, *the mind-body expert Joan Borysenko says*: Joan Borysenko, *Inner Peace for Busy People* (Carlsbad, CA: Hay House Publishing, 2003), 14.

Page 142 *As my wise mentor Carol Orsborn shares from her book* Inner Excellence: Carol Orsborn, *Inner Excellence: Spiritual Principles to Life-Driven Business* (Novato, CA: New World Library, 1993), 97.

CHAPTER 9: BREAKING FREE: MAKING HARD CHOICES

Page 162 *Author Joseph Campbell once said, "Money is congealed energy"*: Joseph Campbell, *A Joseph Campbell Companion: Reflections on the Art of Living*, ed. Diane K. Osbon (1991; reprint, New York: Harper Perennial, 1995), 58.

Page 164 *Robert Puller once said, "Good habits, once established"*: Robert Puller, quoted in Michelle Laverty, *The Secret to Thin Is Within: Motivation for Weight Loss* (Mustang, OK: Tate Publishing, 2011), 124.

CONCLUSION

Page 196 *"May the longtime sun shine upon you"*: "A Very Cellular Song," the Incredible String Band, lyrics by Mike Heron, on *The Hangman's Beautiful Daughter* (Fledg'ling UK), March 1968. The lyrics I quote represent an alternate version of the song that I heard at my son's school. The original version's lyrics slightly differ on the third and fourth lines: "And the pure light within you / Guide you all the way on."

INDEX

INDEX

ABOUT the AUTHOR

Renée Peterson Trudeau is an internationally recognized life balance teacher and speaker. Raised by spiritual seekers, Renée is the oldest of seven Montessori-inspired children. Growing up in Northern California, she attended a yoga school based on the teachings of Parmahansa Yogananada, rode horses bareback and hiked in the vast wilderness of the Sierra Nevada, and learned stained-glass window making and philosophy from the Bhagavad Gita. President of Career Strategists, she has been featured in the *New York Times*, *US News & World Report*, *Good Housekeeping*, and other publications. She is the author of the award-winning *The Mother's Guide to Self-Renewal: How to Reclaim, Rejuvenate and Re-balance Your Life*. Thousands of women in ten countries are joining and being trained to lead Personal Renewal Groups based on her work. Renée is on the faculty of Kripalu Center for Yoga & Health and Esalen Institute, and she speaks and leads life balance workshops/retreats for Fortune 500 companies, conferences, and organizations worldwide. She lives in Austin, Texas, with her husband and son.

Community, resources, and support for nurturing the soul of your family:

- To receive weekly inspiration and resources on how to nurture the soul of your family, join our global community of soulful families at www.Facebook.com/LiveInsideOut.
- Personal Renewal Groups have been nurturing the souls of mothers and families around the world for years. Find out how you can join or become trained to lead these transformative groups at www.ReneeTrudeau.com.
- Interested in scheduling a retreat or workshop for your organization? Choose from one-hour customized workshops to weekend-long retreats. Or, attend one of Renée's public retreats or events. To learn more, visit www.ReneeTrudeau.com.
- Considering a career change or seeking support for enhancing your work/life balance? Check out individual coaching options at www.CareerStrategists.net.